Only in Arkansas

ONLY IN ARKANSAS

A Study of the Endemic
Plants and Animals
of the State

Henry W. Robison
Robert T. Allen

THE UNIVERSITY OF ARKANSAS PRESS

FAYETTEVILLE 1995

99 98 97 96 95   5 4 3 2 1

Designed by Ellen Beeler

⊗ The paper used in this publication meets the minimum requirements of the American National Standard for Permanence of Paper for Printed Library Materials Z39.48-1984.

Library of Congress Cataloging-in-Publication Data

Robison, Henry W.
    Only in Arkansas : a study of the endemic plants and animals of the state / Henry W. Robison, Robert T. Allen.
        p.   cm.
    Includes bibliographical references.
    ISBN 1-55728-326-5 (cloth : alk. paper)
    1. Endemic animals—Arkansas. 2. Endemic plants—Arkansas.   I. Allen, Robert T.   II. Title.
    QL 163.R635   1995
    574.9767—dc20
                                                                                94-35049
                                                                                    CIP

To Patrick and Lindsay, who have waited for years to see their
names in one of my books and who deservedly are listed here
at last, but certainly not least. You have so richly blessed my life
with your lively presence and provided me countless
hours of happiness and joy with your being.
—H. W. Robison

To my wife, Susan M. Allen, in appreciation of
her strong support of my work.
—Robert T. Allen

Acknowledgments

We are indebted to many individuals for providing a variety of assistance during the study. We graciously acknowledge the following for supplying information on localities, taxonomic notes, and/or biology and ecology of the state endemics: Mr. William Shepherd, Dr. Bert Pittman, Harold Grimmet, Arkansas Natural Heritage Commission; Dr. Gary Tucker, FTN and Associates; the late Dr. Horton H. Hobbs Jr., National Museum of Natural History; Dr. Chris Carlton, University of Arkansas; Dr. John Harris, Arkansas Highway and Transportation Department; Mr. David Saugey, U.S. Forest Service; Dr. George L. Harp, Arkansas State University; Dr. Mark E. Gordon, Tennessee Technological University; Mr. James Lynn, Rich Mountain Community College; Dr. Edwin Smith, University of Arkansas; Dr. Barry Poulton, North Texas State University; Mr. Leslie Hubricht, Meridian, Mississippi; Dr. John Holsinger, Old Dominion University; Dr. Edmond J. Bacon, University of Arkansas at Monticello; Dr. Bruce Means, Coastal Plains Institute, Tallahassee, Florida; Dr. John W. Reynolds, Canada; and Dr. Paul Redfearn, Southwest Missouri State University; Dr. Thomas M. Buchanan, Westark Community College, Fort Smith; Mr. Vernon Bates and Mr. Bruce and Lana Ewing, Mena; Dr. Steve Harris and Mr. Kenneth Frazer, Tuscaloosa, Alabama; Dr. Stephen Moulton, North Texas University; Dr. Thomas C. Barr Jr., University of Kentucky; Dr. Thomas E. Bowman, Smithsonian Institution; Dr. Jerry Lewis, Clarksville, Indiana; Ms. Betty G. Cochran, Ms. Mitzi Pardew, U.S. Forest Service.

For use of selected photographs we are indebted to Mr. William Shepherd, Arkansas Natural Heritage Commission; Dr. John Harris, Arkansas Highway and Transportation Department; Mr. Carl Hunter, Little Rock; Dr. Raymond W. Bouchard, Philadelphia Academy of Science; Mr. David Saugey, U.S. Forest Service; Dr. Bruce Bauer, Orlando, Florida; Dr. Bruce Means, Coastal Plains Institute, Florida; Dr. Bill Roston, Forsyth, Missouri; Mr. Vernon Bates, Mena; Mr. David Porter, Kansas City, Missouri; Mr. Neil Compton, Bentonville; Dr. Stan Trauth, Arkansas State University.

Travel funds to complete fieldwork for this book were graciously provided to Henry W. Robison by the Southern Arkansas University Faculty Research Fund.

Contents

Acknowledgments / vii

Arkansas Endemic Biota / xi

1 Introduction / 1

2 An Overview of the State / 15

3 The Plants / 25

4 Phylum Annelida: Segmented Worms / 33

5 Phylum Mollusca: Molluscs / 35

6 Subphylum Crustacea: Crustaceans / 43

7 Myriapoda: Millipedes and Relatives / 63

8 Class Arachnida: Arachnids / 79

9 Class Insecta: Insects / 81

10 Class Osteichthyes: Bony Fishes / 107

11 Class Amphibia: Amphibians / 111

Literature Cited / 113

Index / 119

Arkansas Endemic Biota

I. PLANTS

1. *Plagiochila japonica* Sde. Lac. ex Miquel subspecies *ciliigera*—Liverwort
2. *Arenaria muriculata* Maguire—Sandwort
3. *Carex bicknellii* var. *opaca* F. J. Hermann—Sedge
4. *Delphinium newtonianum* D. M. Moore—Moore's Delphinium
5. *Heuchera villosa* Michx. var. *arkansana* (Rydberg) E. B. Smith—Arkansas Alumroot
6. *Mespilus canescens* Phipps—Stern's Medlar
7. *Quercus shumardi* Buckl. var. *acerifolia* E. J. Palmer—Maple-Leaved Oak
8. *Hydrophyllum brownei* Kral and Bates—Browne's Waterleaf
9. *Cardamine angustata* var. *ouachitana* E. B. Smith—Toothwort
10. *Galium arkansasum* var. *pubiflorum* E. B. Smith
11. *Polymnia cossatotensis* A. B. Pittman and V. Bates—Cossatot Leafcup

II. ANIMALS

A. Annelida (Oligochaeta)—Segmented Worms
1. *Diplocardia meansi* Gates—Earthworm
2. *Diplocardia sylvicola* Gates—Earthworm

B. Mollusca (Gastropoda)—Snails and Slugs
1. *Somatogyrus amnicoloides* Walker—Ouachita Pebblesnail
2. *Somatogyrus crassilabris* Walker—Thicklipped Pebblesnail
3. *Somatogyrus wheeleri* Walker—Channelled Pebblesnail
4. *Amnicola cora* Hubricht—Foushee Cavesnail
5. *Paravitrea aulacogyra* (Pilsbry and Ferriss)—Mt. Magazine Supercoil
6. *Polygyra peregrina* Rehder—White Liptooth
7. *Mesodon clenchi* (Rehder)—Calico Rock Oval
8. *Mesodon magazinensis* (Pilsbry and Ferriss)—Magazine Mountain Shagreen

C. Mollusca (Bivalvia)—Mussels and Clams
1. *Lampsilis powellii* (Lea)—Arkansas Fatmucket
2. *Lampsilis streckeri* Frierson—Speckled Pocketbook
3. *Villosa arkansasensis* (Lea)—Ouachita Creekshell

D. Amphipoda—Amphipods and Scuds
1. *Stygobromus elatus* (Holsinger)—Magazine Mountain Amphipod
2. *Stygobromus montanus* (Holsinger)—Rich Mountain Amphipod

E. Isopoda—Freshwater Isopods and Pill Bugs
1. *Caecidotea fonticulus* Lewis—Abernathy Spring Isopod
2. *Caecidotea holti* Fleming
3. *Lirceus bicuspidatus* Hubricht and Mackin
4. *Lirceus bidentatus* Hubricht and Mackin

F. Decapoda—Shrimps and Crayfishes
1. *Bouchardina robisoni* Hobbs
2. *Cambarus aculabrum* Hobbs and Brown
3. *Cambaris causeyi* Reimer
4. *Cambarus zophonastes* Hobbs and Bedinger
5. *Fallicambarus harpi* Hobbs and Robison
6. *Fallicambarus caesius* Hobbs
7. *Fallicambarus jeanae* Hobbs
8. *Fallicambarus gilpini* Hobbs and Robison
9. *Fallicambarus petilicarpus* Hobbs and Robison
10. *Fallicambarus strawni* (Reimer)
11. *Orconectes acares* Fitzpatrick
12. *Procambarus ferrugineus* Hobbs and Robison
13. *Procambarus liberorum* Fitzpatrick
14. *Procambarus regalis* Hobbs and Robison
15. *Procambarus reimeri* Hobbs

G. Myriapoda—Millipedes and Relatives
1. *Hanseniella ouachiticha* Allen
2. *Desmonus pudicus* (Bollman)
3. *Cibularia profuga* Causey
4. *Mimuloria davidcauseyi* (Causey)
5. *Mimuloria depalmai* (Causey)

6. *Pleuroloma mirbilia* (Causey)
7. *Auturus florus* Causey
8. *Eurymerodesmus angularis* Causey
9. *Eurymerodesmus bentonus* Causey
10. *Eurymerodesmus compressus* Causey
11. *Eurymerodesmus dubius* Chamberlin
12. *Eurymerodesmus goodi* Causey
13. *Eurymerodesmus newtonius* Chamberlin
14. *Eurymerodesmus oliphantus* Chamberlin
15. *Eurymerodesmus schmidti* Chamberlin
16. *Eurymerodesmus wellesleybentonus* Causey
17. *Paresmus columbus* Causey
18. *Paresmus polkensis* Causey
19. *Paresmus pulaski* Causey
20. *Cleidogona arkansana* Causey
21. *Cleidogona aspera* Causey
22. *Ofcookogona alia* Causey
23. *Ofcookogona steuartae* Causey
24. *Ozarkogona glebosa* Causey
25. *Ozarkogona ladymani* Causey
26. *Tiganogona moesta* Causey
27. *Trigenotyla parca* Causey
28. *Craspedosoma flavidum* Bollman
29. *Aliulus carrollus* Causey
30. *Okliulus beveli* Causey
31. *Oriulus grayi* Causey
32. *Cambala arkansana* Chamberlin
33. *Polyzonium bikermani* Causey

H. Pseudoscorpions
1. *Microcreagris ozarkensis* Hoff
2. *Pseudozaona occidentalis* Hoff and Bosterli

I. Diplura—Diplurans
1. *Catajapyx ewingi* Fox
2. *Occasjapyx carltoni* Allen
3. *Podocampa inveterata* Allen
4. *Clivocampa solus* Allen

J. Ephemeroptera—Mayflies
1. *Dannella provonshai* McCafferty
2. *Paraleptophlebia calcarica* Robotham and Allen

K. Plecoptera—Stoneflies
1. *Allocapnia warreni* Ross and Yamamoto
2. *Allocapnia ozarkana* Ross
3. *Allocapnia oribata* Poulton and Stewart

4. *Alloperla ouachita* Stark and Stewart
5. *Alloperla caddo* Poulton and Stewart
6. *Isoperla szczytkoi* Poulton and Stewart
7. *Zealeuctra wachita* Ricker and Ross
8. *Leuctra paleo* Poulton and Stewart

L. Hemiptera—True Bugs
1. *Acalypta susana* Allen, Carlton, and Tedder—Lace Bugs

M. Coleoptera—Beetles
1. *Scaphinotus* (s. str.)*parisiana* Allen and Carlton
2. *Scaphinotus (Nomaretus) infletus* Allen and Carlton
3. *Rhadine ozarkensis* Sanderson and Miller
4. *Evarthus parasodalis* Freitag
5. *Hydroporus sulphurius* Matta and Wolfe
6. *Arianops sandersoni* Barr
7. *Arianops copelandi* Carlton
8. *Ouachitychus parvoculus* Chandler
9. *Pachybrachis pinicola* Rouse and Medvedev—Leaf Beetle
10. *Lema maculicollis* ab. *inornata* Rouse and Medvedev

N. Trichoptera—Caddisflies
1. *Paduniella nearctica* Flint
2. *Paucicalcarica ozarkensis* Matthis and Bowles
3. *Ochrotrichia robisoni* Frazer and Harris
4. *Agapetus medicus* Ross
5. *Helicopsyche limnella* Ross

O. Osteichthyes—Bony Fishes
1. *Noturus lachneri* Taylor—Ouachita Madtom
2. *Noturus taylori* Douglas—Caddo Madtom
3. *Etheostoma moorei* Raney and Suttkus—Yellowcheek Darter
4. *Etheostoma pallididorsum* Distler and Metcalf—Paleback Darter
5. *Etheostoma spectabile fragi* Distler—Strawberry River Orangethroat Darter

P. Amphibia—Frogs, Toads, and Salamanders
1. *Plethodon caddoensis* Pope and Pope—Caddo Mountain Salamander
2. *Plethodon fourchensis* Duncan and Highton—Fourche Mountain Salamander

1

Introduction

Arkansas possesses an incredible diversity of plant and animal life inside its borders. This rich diversity is the result of a varied physiography and topography, a sufficiently long geological history of favorable climates and habitats, periods when the area was isolated from and reconnected with other areas of North America, and the fact that Arkansas was not affected by Pleistocene glaciation during the last one million years.

Within the biological diversity of Arkansas is an element of the biota identifiable as the *endemic* biota —those plants and animals confined to a particular geographic region or area. The Interior Highlands (primarily the Ozark and Ouachita Mountains), for example, have long been recognized as an area of endemism for both plants and animals. As many as three hundred species are known to be endemic to this region of the central United States (Allen, unpub. ms.). For the purpose of this treatise, the political boundaries of Arkansas have been delineated as the *endemic area* to be considered. We are aware of the artificiality of this delineation.

The Arkansas Department of Planning provided the first list of state endemic forms in 1974 in a document that listed 9 endemic species (4 plants, 4 fishes, and 1 salamander) and a detailed account of the state's natural heritage. Later, Robison and Smith (1982) listed 47 taxa as endemic to Arkansas, including 7 plants, 13 crustaceans (2 amphipods, 3 isopods, and 8 crayfishes), 9 insects (1 mayfly, 1 caddisfly, 3 stoneflies, and 4 beetles), 10 snails, 6 fishes, and 2 salamanders. Allen (1988b) added yet another 39 forms to the list of state endemics. Papers published during the last few years describing a number of new endemic species show that there is still a considerable amount of work to be done before we can accurately enumerate Arkansas's endemic biota. Endemic forms play a vital role in our state's natural heritage because they represent those

biological entities whose entire populations have been fortuitously delineated within Arkansas's political boundaries.

In this treatise, we document a total of 117 taxa (species and subspecies) of plants and animals as endemic to the state of Arkansas, including 11 plants (1 bryophyte and 10 flowering plants) and 106 animals. The animal forms are dominated by 99 invertebrates, which include 2 annelid worms, 8 snails, 3 mussels, 21 crustaceans (2 amphipods, 4 isopods, and 15 crayfishes), 33 myriapods (millipedes, centipedes, and symphylans), 2 pseudoscorpions, and 30 insects (4 diplurans, 2 mayflies, 5 caddisflies, 8 stoneflies, 10 beetles, and 1 true bug). Seven vertebrates are state endemics represented by 5 fishes and 2 salamanders.

This book has been prepared to (1) serve as a compilation of all of those fauna and flora deemed endemic to Arkansas; (2) provide pertinent literature references to the original distributions of each form within the state; and (3) report what is known of the general biology, evolutionary relationships, and habitat occupied by each endemic form.

It is hoped that the exposure to the general public of these life forms as endemic to the state will stimulate future research and preservation. The Arkansas endemics are important to understanding the origin of the North American biota and its evolution during the past 600 million years of history; however, we currently know little about these state treasures. The preliminary data indicate that the Interior Highlands, including north and west Arkansas, provided a safe haven for many forms during geological epochs when most of the rest of the continent was not available for habitation. During these times of isolation many forms evolved into new species.

The discussion of endemic species will never be

FIG. 1.1. An example of the maple-leaved oak (*Quercus shumardi* Buckl. var. *acerifolia*) growing near Brown Springs on Magazine Mountain. *Photograph by Robert T. Allen.*

completed or finalized because new species are continually being discovered within the state. As collecting continues in the remote mountainous regions of Arkansas, the list of Arkansas endemics will most certainly increase. Because of their special intrinsic value to Arkansas, protection of all forms endemic to the state is strongly urged.

The Importance of Endemic Species

Endemic species are organisms that occur only in a particular area. The area may be very large, such as the North American continent, or very small, such as a single freshwater spring or mountaintop. An endemic area may also be defined by natural boundaries, as in the case of the Interior Highlands (the geological formations of the Ozark and Ouachita Mountains), or it may be more artificial, as in political boundaries.

There are psychological, practical, and scientific reasons for an interest in what is unique and different. Outstanding national attractions occurring within a state are a source of pride and are often a valuable economic resource. For instance, thousands of people travel each year to Wyoming to see bison and elk in their native habitats.

In Arkansas we have a fairly large number of species of plants and animals that live only in the state. One example of such an endemic species is the maple-leaved oak (*Quercus shumardi* Buckl. var. *acerifolia*), a

tree that lives only on Magazine Mountain in Logan County (fig. 1.1). For the most part, our unique endemic plants and animals are more obscure and less well known than bison, elk, and whooping cranes. Nevertheless, our endemic species are just as important as better-known and more visible species, and we should give serious consideration to making the general public more aware of them.

Local endemic species may be indicators of natural phenomena worthy of preservation. A number of endemic species, including the Magazine Mountain shagreen snail are on the federal list of endangered and threatened species and thus protected by law. Many of us recall that some years ago a small fish, the snail darter, held up construction of a multimillion-dollar dam in Tennessee. Sizable blocks of land must frequently be purchased in order to provide protection, and conservation organizations must engender interest and raise money to acquire such land.

Endemic species generate a multitude of questions and present a host of possibilities for scientists to learn more about nature. One of the most obvious questions is "Why do endemic species occur in a particular area or habitat?" The answer to this question is seldom obvious, and the search for the answer is often fraught with frustration and long, painstaking hours of research. Frequently, postulated theories are incomplete or false, and essential pertinent data is absent in related fields of science. Nevertheless, unique organisms are usually the first to attract the attention of biologists and the amateur naturalists. Let us consider, in depth, what scientists can learn about natural history from a study of endemic species.

Relatives and Long-Distance Connections

Just as human families sometimes become scattered in many states or countries and separated by great distances, even oceans, so do plants and animals. By compiling a family genealogy, many of us can trace our family origins back to Europe, Africa, Asia, or some other distant land. When we study the distribution of plants and animals, including their evolutionary and geographic relationships, we call the science *biogeography*. Some of the endemic plants and animals of Arkansas have their closest relatives in the eastern or western mountains of North America or in such distant lands as Korea and Japan. Let us consider some of the biotic connections and offer a tentative explanation for these long-distance connections.

The science of biogeography began in the early part of the 1800s when a French botanist, A. P. de Candolle (1830), studied plants on a worldwide basis. De Candole noticed that while most plant species were confined to one continent (continental endemics), many of these species did have certain curious distant relationships with plants on other continents. An ornithologist, P. L. Sclater (1858), also recognized that different continents had, for the most part, different species of birds. Sclater published his observation in a paper entitled "On the General Geographic Distribution of the Members of the Class Aves" in 1858. After making an extensive list of bird species in different parts of the world, Sclater suggested that the world could be divided into six major biological areas. Alfred Wallace (1876) extended the work of Sclater to include many other animal groups and recognized what became known as the world's six zoological realms. These "realms" were essentially the major continental areas: North America, South America, Europe, Africa, Asia, and Australia (fig. 1.2).

Since the time of Sclater and Wallace we have made great strides in biogeographic studies. We now have a much more complete knowledge of the distribution of many plant and animal species. We also have a good understanding of the major geological events that affected the distribution of plants and animals. But, in some ways biogeographers are still struggling with definitively establishing distribution patterns and explaining how these patterns came about. Some of the endemic species in Arkansas are extremely informative and can teach us a great deal about regional, continental, and even worldwide distribution patterns.

Arkansas plant and animal species can be divided into three general groups: (1) species with a more or less continuous range in areas outside the state, but including Arkansas; (2) species having what are called *disjunct distributions;* and (3) the endemic species found only in Arkansas.

By far, the majority of Arkansas's plants and animals have ranges that occur outside the state's boundaries. Some of these ranges are extensive, such as the American robin (*Turdus migratorius*), whose range encompasses much of North America; the slimy salamander complex (*Plethodon glutinosus* complex) (fig. 1.3); and the shagbark hickory (*Carya ovata* [Mill.] K. Koch) (fig. 1.4). Other species, such as Ozark witch

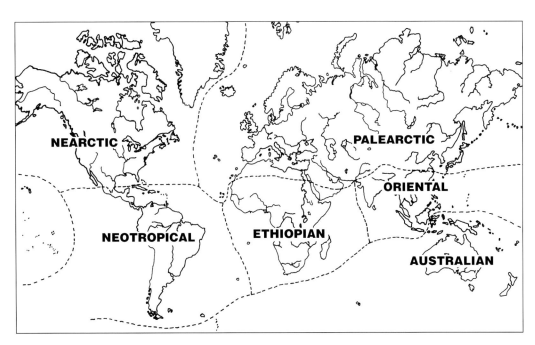

FIG. 1.2. The six zoological realms established by P. L. Sclater and confirmed by A. R. Wallace during the 1800s. These two early naturalists found that most species within each realm were endemics. *Redrawn from Darlington 1957.*

hazel (*Hamamelis vernalis* Serg.) (fig. 1.5), Ozark spiderwort (*Tradescantia ozarkana* Anderson and Woodson) (fig. 1.6), and the ground beetle (*Evarthrus whitcombi* Freitag) (fig. 1.7), have ranges that occur outside of Arkansas but are confined to the Interior Highlands.

Disjunct species are those forms that have noticeable geographical gaps in their distribution ranges. Examples of species with disjunct distributions in at least part of Arkansas are yellowwood (*Cladrastis lutea* [Michx.] K. Koch) (fig. 1.8) and the queen snake (*Regina septemvittata*) (fig. 1.9).

The endemic species discussed in this book occur only in Arkansas. Arkansas endemics are interesting because they represent clues about specialized habitats and they are possible keys to unlocking some bit of information about the past natural history of the region. These locally occurring endemic species may be instructive in learning about biological phenomena; if we are extremely lucky, they may lead us to the discovery of a new biological phenomenon or law. Arkansas endemic species already reveal specific information about ancient geographical biotic relationships.

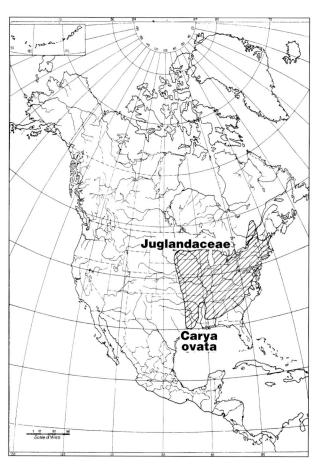

FIG. 1.4. Distribution of shagbark hickory (*Carya ovata* [Mill.] K. Koch) in North America.

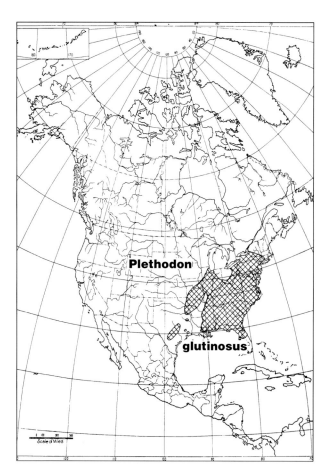

FIG. 1.3. Distribution of the slimy salamander (*Plethodon glutinosus* complex) in North America.

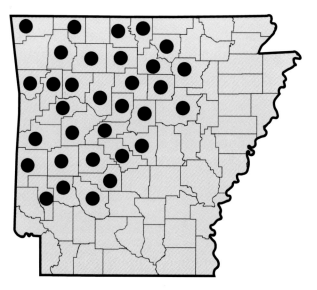

FIG. 1.5. Ozark witch hazel (*Hamamelis vernalis* Serg.) is an endemic species of the Interior Highlands.

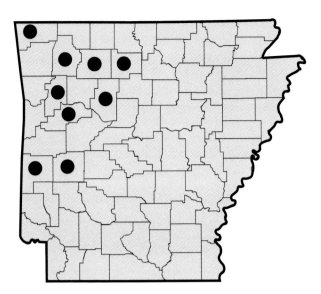

FIG. 1.6. Ozark spiderwort (*Tradescantia ozarkana* Anderson and Woodson), another Interior Highlands endemic, is widely distributed in Arkansas, but also occurs in a few counties in Missouri.

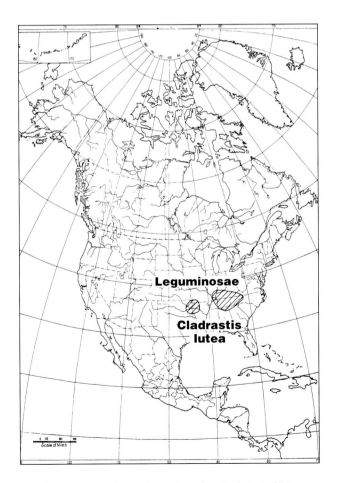

FIG. 1.8. Yellowwood (*Cladrastis lutea* [Michx.] K. Koch) is an example of a species with a disjunct distribution east and west of the Mississippi River.

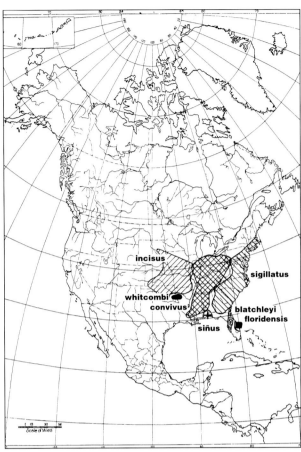

FIG. 1.7. The ground beetle (*Evarthrus whitcombi* Freitag) is endemic to the Ouachita Mountains of Arkansas and Oklahoma. Its close relative, *Evarthrus incisus* Freitag, occurs mostly north of the Arkansas River valley. Other related species are isolated east of the Mississippi River. *Modified from Freitag 1969.*

Long-Distance Connections in North America

If you have ever visited the Appalachian Mountains in the east, you have no doubt noticed the similarity in vegetation between that area (below 3,500 feet) and many hillsides in Arkansas. If one were blindfolded and taken to the northwest-facing slope of Magazine Mountain in Logan County, it would be difficult, at least at first glance, for him to determine whether he was near Gatlinburg, Tennessee, or Paris, Arkansas (fig. 1.10). Even the terrain and climate are similar, as well as the animals. When we examine this similarity critically, particularly in reference to endemic species, we find excellent scientific evidence of ancient biotic connections between the two areas.

Living on Magazine Mountain is a very small short-winged mold beetle, about 0.25 inch long, whose

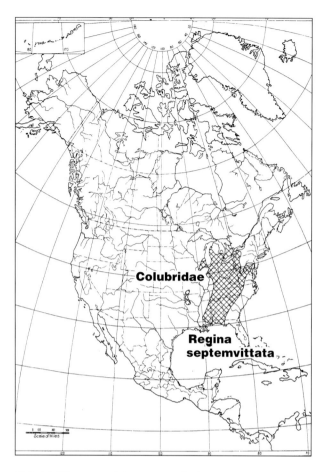

FIG. 1.9. The range of the queen snake (*Regina septemvittata*) occurs mostly east of the Mississippi River valley, but there is a disjunct population on the western side of the Interior Highlands.

scientific name is *Arianops sandersoni* Barr (family Pselaphidae) (fig. 1.11). A female of this species was collected in 1949 by Milton Sanderson of the Illinois Natural History Survey, but the species was not formally described and named until 1972 by Thomas Barr of the University of Kentucky. One of the interesting facts about this beetle is where its nearest relatives occur, which is the Appalachian Mountains some five hundred miles away. Barr's treatise on the genus *Arianops* listed thirty-two species from the Appalachians and one species isolated in Arkansas. (We now know that there are three or more *Arianops* species in the Ouachita Mountains). There are no known intervening populations between these two areas (fig. 1.12).

While searching for additional specimens of the short-winged mold beetle in 1985, entomologists from the University of Arkansas found yet another new beetle species on the slopes of Magazine Mountain. This beetle was rather large, 1.5 inches long, and belonged to a group commonly called Ground Beetles (family Carabidae). Eventually, the new beetle was named *Scaphinotus parisiana* Allen and Carlton (1989) (fig. 1.13.) It is also known from near Fayetteville in Washington County. Both the feeding habits and the distribution of close relatives of *Scaphinotus parisiana* are interesting.

Scaphinotus parisiana belongs to a group of beetles that feed exclusively on escargot. The heads of these beetles have become elongate to accommodate their feeding practices; once they take hold of a snail,

FIG. 1.10. Mountainside vegetation (a) near Gatlinburg, Tennessee, and (b) near Paris, Arkansas. *Photographs by Robert T. Allen.*

FIG. 1.11. This short-winged mold beetle (*Arianops sandersoni* Barr) is known to occur only on Magazine Mountain. *Photograph by Robert T. Allen.*

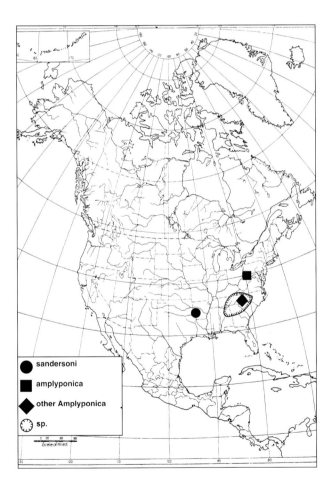

FIG. 1.12. There are thirty-two species in the beetle genus *Arianops* (family Pselaphidae) that occur in the Appalachian highlands and two, possible three, species in the Ouachita Mountains of Arkansas and Oklahoma. *Based on data from Barr 1974.*

FIG. 1.13. This snail-feeding beetle (*Scaphinotus parisiana* Allen and Carlton) was first discovered on Magazine Mountain in 1986. Other specimens were later found near Fayetteville, Washington County. *Photograph by Robert T. Allen.*

they are able to push their narrow head into the snail's shell and consume the entire animal. Of the fifteen North American species that belong to the same subgroup as the Arkansas species, fourteen occur outside of Arkansas: "three [occur in the] mountains of northern Mexico; eight [in the] mountains of New Mexico and southern Arizona; three [in the] Appalachian mountain system and adjacent lowlands, northward to southern Quebec" (Ball 1973) (fig. 1.14). One additional species, *elevatus*, also occurs in Arkansas. Unlike its relatives, this species inhabits lowland areas throughout eastern North America.

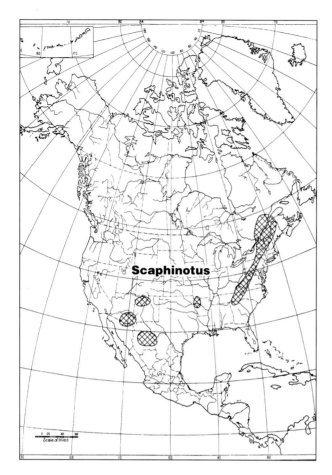

FIG. 1.14. Snail-feeding beetles in the genus *Scaphinotus* are found isolated in the mountains of Mexico and in the United States in New Mexico, Arizona, Arkansas, and the Appalachian Mountains. *Based on data from Ball 1973.*

Arkansas endemic insects are not the only animals that have close relationships with Appalachian forms. There are at least two endemic species of salamanders in the genus *Plethodon* that occur only in Arkansas (*P. caddoensis* and *P. fourchensis*) that have Appalachian relatives. Both of these species are confined to the Ouachita Mountains in the extreme western part of the state.

In the ground beetle and *Plethodon* examples just discussed, there are not only Arkansas-Appalachian relationships, but also intracontinental east-west relationships. We noted that the snail-feeding beetles were found in mountains in Mexico and the southwestern United States. In addition to Appalachia and the Ozark/Ouachita uplift, the genus *Plethodon* is also found in southwest Texas, a small area in Idaho and Wyoming, and in the Pacific Northwest (fig. 1.15). As we shall presently see, these broad east-west patterns that embrace the entire continent are relevant to understanding the natural history of Arkansas.

Biotic connections between Arkansas plants and

animals and those in the west are not as numerous as the Arkansas-Appalachian connections. In recent years biologists have begun to discover a few Arkansas–western North American connections. One such western connection was recently found to exist in an ancient wingless group of insects called Diplura (they have no common name). In this case a new species was collected by C. E. Carlton near the Buffalo River in Newton County. This species was found to belong to the genus *Occasjapyx* and was described and named *Occasjapyx carltoni* Allen (fig. 1.16). The only other known occurrence of this genus is the presence of five species in California (fig. 1.17). Thus, it would appear that there may be Arkansas species whose ancient and nearest relatives live in western North America.

Worldwide Long-Distance Connections

The extended east-west biotic connections that some Arkansas species have are important in studying the

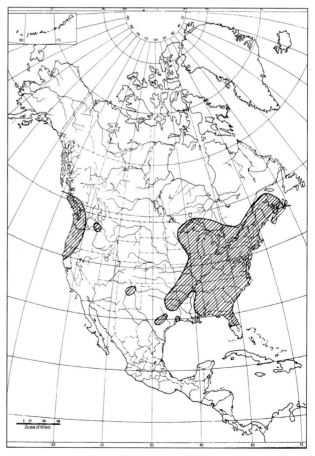

FIG. 1.15. The North American distribution of the salamander genus *Plethodon* consists of isolated populations of endemic species reaching from coast to coast. *Redrawn from Highton 1962.*

FIG.1.16. *Occasjapyx carltoni* Allen is a dipluran, which are wingless, blind insects that live under rocks in moist, cool areas. They are the most ancient living insects. This species is known from a single locality near the Buffalo River in Newton County. *Photograph by Robert T. Allen.*

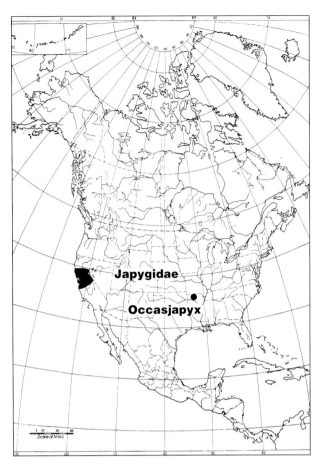

FIG. 1.17. The Arkansas endemic *Occasjapyx carltoni* is closely related to other species in the genus known only from California.

biogeography of organisms in North America. Species that are endemic to Arkansas and the Interior Highlands have connections that literally reach around the globe. Although this book is predominantly about Arkansas endemics, we feel it is important to consider these Arkansas endemics in relation to an increasing order of geographical magnitude (i.e., biotic/geographic relationships within Arkansas, within the Interior Highlands, within North America, and, ultimately, globally). Two examples from the insects serve as examples of Arkansas's global connections.

Milton Sanderson, who discovered the short-winged mold beetle on Magazine Mountain, discovered another new beetle living in the crevices of Devil's Den State Park. The Devil's Den discovery was a rove beetle called *Rimulinkola divalis* Sanderson (1946) (fig. 1.18). This small beetle, about 0.25 inch long, was so strikingly different that it was placed in its own genus, *Rimulinkola*. For over thirty years, the beetle was known only from Devil's Den State Park. However, extensive collecting during the late sixties and into the seventies showed the beetle to be fairly common throughout the Ozark/Ouachita area; yet, it has never been collected outside of the Interior Highlands. Further studies on the anatomy and morphology of his species also revealed that *divalis* belonged to the genus *Derops*, not *Rimulinkola*. It is the only representative of this genus in North America. The other species of *Derops* occur all the way around the globe in Japan and northern China. This is a most remarkable worldwide distribution pattern.

Another global distribution pattern in the caddisfly genus *Paduniella* was discovered by Oliver Flint

(1967), who works at the United States National Museum in Washington, D.C. From a collection of insects, again from Devil's Den State Park, Flint recognized, described, and named the species *Paduniella nearctica* Flint. Flint's Nearctic caddisfly is the only representative of this genus and the subfamily (Paduniellinae) in North America. The closest relative of this species occurs on the island of Sri Lanka (Ceylon) at the southern tip of India (fig.1.19). Other species in the group occur in many parts of Asia.

It is obvious from the studies that have been made that the Arkansas biota is not only rich in species numbers, but it also has a most interesting history reaching back in time some 300 million years. We certainly do not have all the answers relevant to understanding this history, but we can offer a tentative outline of what may have happened.

During the past four decades biologists and earth scientists have learned a great deal about the 600-million-year history of our planet. Here we outline some of the major events that have taken place in

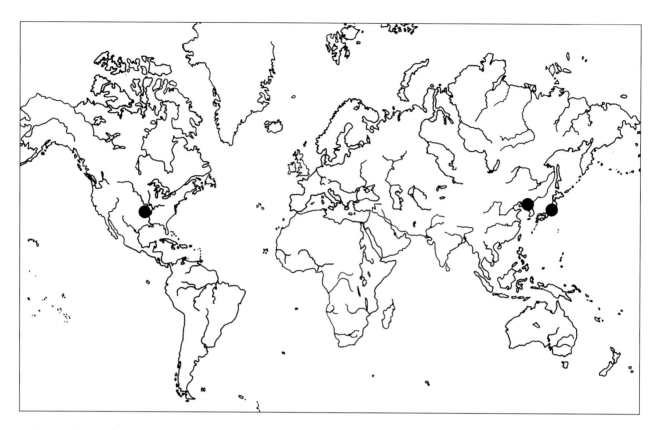

FIG. 1.18. The rove beetle *Derops divalis* Sanderson and Miller is found throughout the Interior Highlands from southern Illinois to eastern Oklahoma. The closest relatives of this beetle are found in northern Asia.

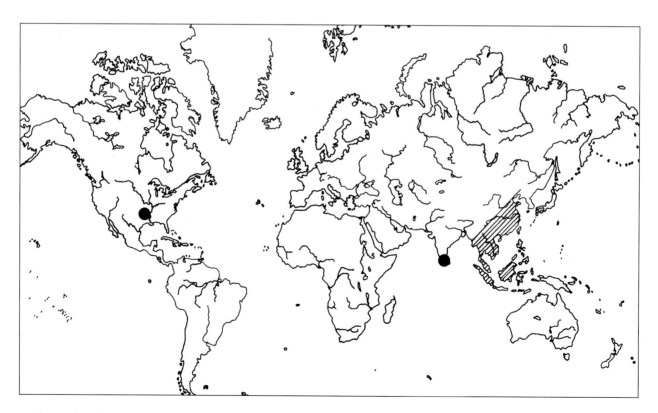

FIG. 1.19. The Arkansas endemic caddisfly *Paduniella nearctica* is the only North American representative of the subfamily to which this species belongs. Its nearest relative occurs on the island of Sri Lanka (Ceylon). Other species in the group are found in Asia. *Based on data from Flint 1967.*

relation to our own small segment of the world. This outline will give the reader a basic idea of how some of the earth's events played a role in shaping the present-day biota of Arkansas.

Earth scientists have shown beyond doubt that the vast land areas we call continents rest on continental plates, and these plates have been moving over the surface of our planet for eons. During the Triassic (230 mya) all the continents were together and formed one large landmass, Pangea (fig. 1.20A). During the Jurassic (180 mya), the period after the Triassic, North America, Europe, and northern Asia broke away from Pangea but remained connected to one another (fig. 1.20A). These three continents began to move northward to form a large landmass called Laurasia. The southern landmass is called Gondwana. During the Cretaceous (100 mya), the Gondwana continent began to drift apart.

During the Cretaceous and extending into the Eocene (49 mya), North America, Europe, and northern Asia remained united. There were, however, vast epicontinental seas that effectively divided the northern segment, Laurasia, into isolated segments (figs. 1.21, 1.22). One such sea was called the Mid-Continental Seaway, which divided eastern and western North America. Another seaway, the Tergai Sea, divided Europe from Northern Asia (fig. 1.22). Thus, these epicontinental seas divided Laurasia into two, possibly three, major above-water landmasses: eastern North America was united with Europe (Euroamerica) and western North America *may have been* united with northern Asia across Alaska (Asia-america). Movement of plants and animals within the land-connected areas was possible, but the fossil record indicates there was little movement across the seaways. Thus, Europe and North America had a communal biota during much of the Cretaceous.

During the Cretaceous much of the world's biota began to change radically. Dinosaurs became extinct at the end of the Cretaceous and mammals proliferated and eventually became a dominant group. The first occurrences of flowering plants, angiosperms, are found in the Cretaceous fossil record. From these early flowering plants developed the northern temperate deciduous forests. Data from the fossil record suggest that the first temperate deciduous forest reached around the globe in the northern latitudes.

During the beginning epochs of the Tertiary (the Paleocene, Eocene, and Oligocene, 63 to 25 mya) the earth's climate was in a state of flux: sometimes warming, sometimes cooling. The epicontinental seas also receded from the land for the most part. During the cooler periods, elements of the northern deciduous forest shifted their ranges southward. Also, during the

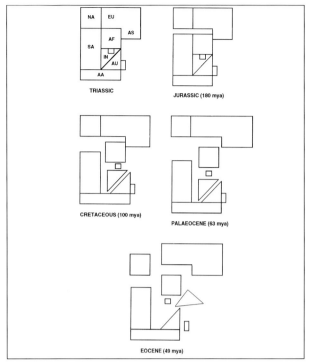

A

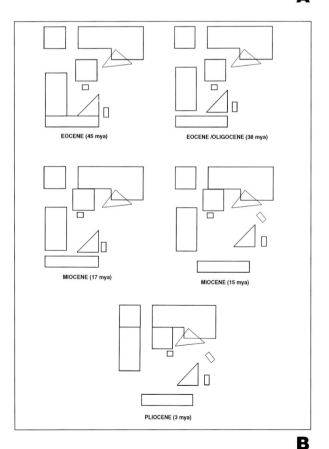

B

FIG. 1.20. A schematic representation of the position and separation times of the continents from the Triassic period (230 mya) until the present.

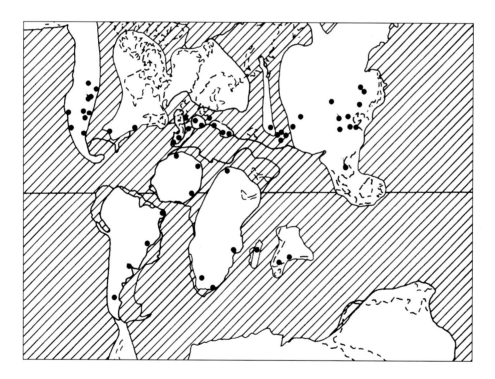

FIG. 1.21. During the first part of the Cretaceous period (135 mya), North America, Europe, and northern Asia had separated from the continents in the Southern Hemisphere. Based on the fossil record, Cox (1974) has suggested that Europe and North America were connected by land but were separated from northern Asia by an epicontinental seaway known as the Turgai Seaway or Tergai Straits. *From Cox 1974.*

FIG. 1.22. By the latter part of the Cretaceous (90 mya), an epicontinental seaway had invaded North America, separating the eastern and western parts of the continent. Eastern North America was still connected to Europe by land. *From Cox 1974.*

Eocene (49 mya) North America and Europe drifted apart, opening the North Atlantic Ocean (fig. 1.20B). The drifting continents, climatic changes, and movement southward of the deciduous forest, in effect, divided the deciduous forest into three major units: eastern North America, Europe, and northern Asia (principally northern China, Taiwan, Korea, and Japan). If this scenario is correct, then it is not difficult to see how the now-isolated groups in eastern North America, including Arkansas, have close relatives on the opposite side of the earth.

The theory previously outlined may seem fanciful to some readers; however, the geological data, fossil data, and data from present-day distributions all point in the same direction—the plants and animals of the Northern Hemisphere continents must have been connected at one time. Eastern North America, Europe, and northern Asia share hundreds of genera and families. When one tabulates the number of shared groups between the areas, a repetitious pattern emerges. Scientists believe that where one finds congruent, repetitious patterns, there are logical, scientific explanations for the patterns.

The part Arkansas biota has played, and will play, in adding data to our understanding of the earth's history cannot be overestimated. The state contains an inordinate number of rare and unique species that are significant parts of the historical picture of our world.

Using This Book

The outline of this book is arranged hierarchically according to the classifications found in most general biology texts and in field guides. The plants are considered first and then the animals. Within each of these large groups, the forms that are thought to have the most primitive or ancestral set of characteristics are considered first. For example, millipedes are thought to be more primitive, in many ways, than insects. Thus, the chapter on millipedes precedes the chapter on insects.

A typical hierarchy consists of a number of ascending, more inclusive categories or taxa. The least inclusive category is the subspecies. The maple-leaved oak (*Quercus shumardi acerifolia*) is a subspecies of Shumards oak (*Quercus shumardi shumardi*). The most inclusive category used here is the kingdom. For reference, a typical hierarchy is shown here:

Kingdom: Animalia—Animals
    Phylum: Arthropoda—spiders, millipedes, insects, etc.
    Class: Insecta—insects
    Order: Coleoptera—beetles
    Family: Pselaphidae—short-winged mold beetles
    Genus: *Arianops*—no common name
    Species: *sandersoni*—no common name

Where possible we have used common names. But, in many instances, as in the example just given, a common name is not available. This is especially true for most species of arthropods. The scientific names are not all that difficult to pronounce. Generally, the reader can "sound out" scientific names and pronounce them correctly. Long before they enter the first grade, children raised by avid collectors and naturalists are reporting Carabidae for ground beetles, Papilionidae for swallowtail butterflies, and *Turdus migratoris* for American robins in the backyard.

Under each species the following information is provided: (1) the scientific name followed by the last name of the person(s) who described the species, the year described, and the page number on which the name first appears in the original description; (2) the common name, if any; (3) type depository, the institution where the single specimen resides, which is used for all final references; (4) type locality, usually the place where the species was first collected; (5) distribution records, the counties in Arkansas from which specimens have been collected; and (6) a discussion of general and specific information that is known about the species.

The extent of the discussion section under each species varies. In the case of the millipedes, we know practically nothing about the biology of the species. In many instances the millipede species listed here have not been collected since the original specimens were found.

A majority of the Arkansas endemic species occur in the Ozark and Ouachita Mountains. This, we believe, is not due to less collecting in the lowland areas of the state, but rather to the geological history of Arkansas and to the fact that many forms become isolated in mountainous regions. Also, a number of new species which are currently recognized but are technically undescribed by taxonomic specialists are known to us to be state endemics, for example Ouachita darter (*Percina sp. nov*). These were purposely omitted in this treatise because they lacked official taxonomic status.

We sincerely hope that this book will provide an impetus for a greater appreciation of the natural heritage of Arkansas and a foundation for future studies on the endemic flora and fauna of the state. The preservation and protection of natural habitats become more critical each day. The greater our knowledge about Arkansas's biota, the more wisely we will be able to use our monetary resources to preserve these unique forms.

2

An Overview of the State

Arkansas has a diverse topography, with lowlands and swamps in the eastern and southern part of the state and sizable mountains with steep cliffs and deep, protected valleys in the north and west. Arkansas has over 600,000 acres of lakes and 20,000 miles of streams (Robison and Smith, 1984) (fig. 2.1). There are five major river systems—the Arkansas, White, St. Francis, Ouachita, and Mississippi Rivers—with numerous tributaries (fig. 2.2). Both the White and Ouachita Rivers have their sources in the state. The climate is variable with the northwestern corner of the state usually receiving considerably more snow than the southeast. All of these factors and others make it possible for many different kinds of plants and animals to find suitable habitats in Arkansas. Over time, the plants and animals have sorted themselves out into identifiable communities. Within these communities, we are able to detect one or more endemic species.

The various assemblages of plants and animals, the topography, and the evolution of distinct, endemic species in Arkansas did not occur overnight. These physical and biotic factors are the result of hundreds of millions of years of evolutionary history.

Natural Regions of Arkansas

Arkansas can easily be divided into six rather distinct natural physiographic regions: the Ozark Mountains, the Ouachita Mountains, the Arkansas Valley, the West Gulf Coastal Plain, the Mississippi Alluvial Plain (Delta), and Crowley's Ridge (figs. 2.3, 2.4). These six areas are delineated by a combination of their geological substrate, topography, animals, and vegetation.

Ozark Mountains

The Ozark Mountains occupy most of northwestern and north central Arkansas and are characterized by rugged, flat-topped mountains, long, deep valleys, steep cliffs and ledges, and clear, spring-fed streams. Elevations range from 250 to 2,450 feet (76 to 747 m) above sea level. This region has been above sea level since the Pennsylvanian period, more than 300 million years ago. Principal rock types are Ordovician limestone and dolomite, Pennsylvanian sandstone, and Pennsylvanian and Ordovician shales. Soils are primarily residual and vegetation is primarily upland hardwood forests of white oak, red oak, and hickory (fig. 2.5).

The Ozark Mountains natural region is made up of three distinct topographic subdivisions: the Salem

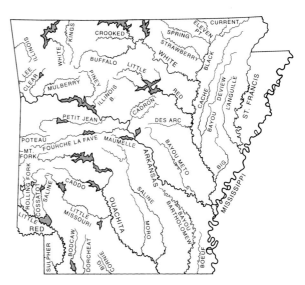

FIG. 2.1. Major rivers, streams, and lakes in Arkansas.

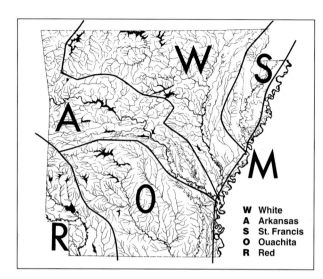

FIG. 2.2. Major river systems in Arkansas.

W White
A Arkansas
S St. Francis
O Ouachita
R Red

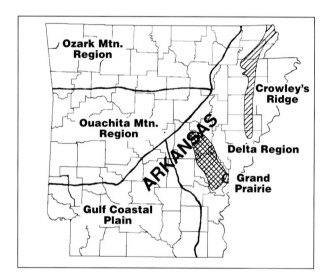

FIG. 2.3. Physiographic regions of Arkansas.

Plateau, the Springfield Plateau, and the Boston Mountains.

Ouachita Mountains

The Ouachita Mountains compose a belt about 60 miles (96.5 km) wide and 120 (193 km) miles long that was subjected to intensive structural movements that warped, twisted, and folded beds of rock. The mountains exist today as a series of east-west trending ridges with elevations up to 2,681 feet (818 m) above sea level on Rich Mountain near Mena.

The Ouachita Mountain province may be divided into three subprovinces: the Fourche Mountains to the north, the "Novaculite Uplift" or Central Ouachita Mountains, and the Athens Piedmont to the south.

Principal rock types are Paleozoic sedimentary sandstones, shales, and novaculites ranging in age from Ordovician to Pennsylvanian. Most of the soils are derived from shale and sandstone and belong to the sandy loam group. Typical vegetation includes short-leaf pine and upland and lowland hardwood forests (fig. 2.6).

Arkansas Valley (Arkhoma Basin)

The Arkansas Valley, also called the Arkhoma Basin (fig. 2.7), is a deep trough lying between the Ozark Mountains to the north and the Ouachita Mountains to the south. The valley contains the youngest Paleozoic rock in Arkansas and is characterized by rolling plains 500 to 600 feet (152 to 183 m) above sea level and 25 to 30 miles (40 to 48 km) wide from Searcy in White County west to Ft. Smith. Interestingly, within this

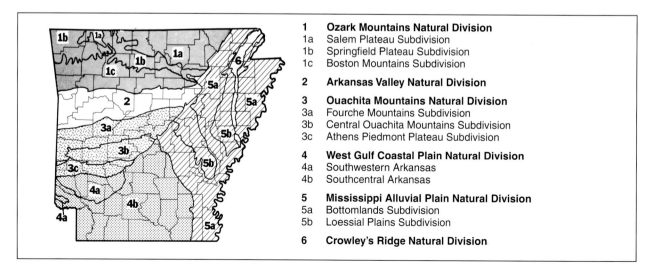

1	**Ozark Mountains Natural Division**
1a	Salem Plateau Subdivision
1b	Springfield Plateau Subdivision
1c	Boston Mountains Subdivision
2	**Arkansas Valley Natural Division**
3	**Ouachita Mountains Natural Division**
3a	Fourche Mountains Subdivision
3b	Central Ouachita Mountains Subdivision
3c	Athens Piedmont Plateau Subdivision
4	**West Gulf Coastal Plain Natural Division**
4a	Southwestern Arkansas
4b	Southcentral Arkansas
5	**Mississippi Alluvial Plain Natural Division**
5a	Bottomlands Subdivision
5b	Loessial Plains Subdivision
6	**Crowley's Ridge Natural Division**

FIG. 2.4. The major natural divisions of Arkansas.

FIG. 2.5. Ozark Mountains. *Photograph by Robert T. Allen.*

FIG. 2.6. Ouachita Mountains. *Photograph by Robert T. Allen.*

FIG. 2.7. Arkansas Valley (Arkhoma Basin). *Photograph by Robert T. Allen.*

FIG. 2.8. West Gulf Coastal Plain. *Photograph by Robert T. Allen.*

FIG. 2.9. Mississippi Alluvial Plain. *Photograph by Robert T. Allen.*

FIG. 2.10. Crowley's Ridge. *Photograph by Robert T. Allen.*

rolling lowland are isolated flat-topped, mesa-like mountains such as Mount Nebo, Petit Jean Mountain, and the highest point in Arkansas, Magazine Mountain (2753 feet; 853 m).

West Gulf Coastal Plain

The West Gulf Coastal Plain was once covered by the Gulf of Mexico 50 million years ago. It is divided into two regions: southwest Arkansas and southcentral Arkansas. The area is characterized by level to rolling areas, hilly sections, numerous bottoms, and occasional prairies. Elevations vary from 59 feet (18 m) (the lowest in the state) to about 700 feet (213 m). A variety of soils, including marl, chalk, sandstone, and shale, occur in this area with clay, gravel, and silt being common (fig. 2.8).

Mississippi Alluvial Plain

Eastern Arkansas is included in the Delta natural division. The Mississippi Alluvial Plain is a part of the

Coastal Plain that the Mississippi River and its tributaries formed. Elevations average only 100 to 300 feet (30.5 to 91.5 m) above sea level. The alluvium deposited by the Arkansas and Mississippi Rivers makes this region the richest and most fertile of Arkansas. The Coastal Plain is basically subdivided into smaller plains, which are predominantly ancient river terraces or soils derived from rocks and the bottomlands, which are predominantly recent floodplains (fig. 2.9).

Crowley's Ridge

Crowley's Ridge is a long, narrow area of rolling hills that ranges from 1 to 10 miles (1.6 to 16 km) wide and runs from southern Missouri to Helena, Arkansas (fig. 2.10). The Ridge is 100 to 250 feet (30 to 76 m) above the surrounding alluvial plain; it represents an ancient divide between the Mississippi and Ohio Rivers when the Mississippi flowed west of the Ridge and the Ohio flowed east of it. Crowley's Ridge is made up of loessial (wind blown) soils which are older than the surrounding alluvium. Because of the nature of the soils, the ridge is subject to extensive and severe erosion resulting in deep gullies and ravines. The vegetation that occurs on Crowley's Ridge is more closely related to the flora (tulip tree–oak forests) of Tennessee than to the oak hickory forests of the Ozarks. This indicates that the biota of Crowley's Ridge had a more recent connection with the Tennessee biota than with the biota of the Ozark/Ouachita area in Arkansas.

A Brief Geological History of Arkansas

The six natural regions of Arkansas are the result of some 320 million years of earth history. It will be helpful if we briefly discuss what was going on during various time intervals in the area we now call Arkansas. To do this we will use the time scale geologists employ to divide the earth's history into intervals (fig. 2.11). This geological time scale puts into perspective the relationships of events in geological history.

Before the Pennsylvanian era, Arkansas was covered with sea water. We know this because in many areas of the state there are excellent deposits containing the remains of sea animals, such as trilobites (now extinct), sharks teeth, and clams. But during the Pennsylvanian era, the first of many major cataclysms took place in Arkansas. The Ozark Mountains arose

and protruded high above the surrounding epicontinental seas. Geologists are not certain what caused this uplift, but it appears that a large area reaching from southern Illinois across southern Missouri and into northern Arkansas and eastern Oklahoma was pushed up enmass. How high the uplift may have once been is also uncertain. The area, however, was never again

CENOZOIC-*Modern life*		
Quaternary		
Pleistocene	1	The ice ages to the present
Tertiary		
Pliocene	13	Large carnivores
Miocene	25	Dominance of flowering plants
Oligocene	36	Diversification of mammals
Eocene	58	Radiation of placental mammals
Paleocene	63	First placental mammals
MESOZOIC-*Medieval life*		
Cretaceous	135	Dominance of cycads (tropical trees)
Jurassic	181	Ferns and conifers
Triassic	230	Dinosaurs
PALEOZOIC-*Ancient life*		
Permian	280	Evolution of modern insect orders
Pennsylvanian	310	The Carboniferous tropical
Mississippian	345	forests
Devonian	405	Beginnings of land animals
Silurian	425	Predominance of marine inverte-
Ordovician	500	brates; rise of land plants
Cambrian	? 600	

Origin of universe   about 13–20,000,000,000

Origin of oldest known stars   6,500,000,000

Origin of solar system   5,000,000,000

Origin of earth   4,500,000,000

Origin of continents and final cool stage   3,500,000,000

Origin of life   2,000,000,000

Origin of oxidizing atmosphere   1,000,000,000

First well-marked fossil beds of Paleozoic era   over 600,000,000

FIG. 2.11. A standard geological time scale in millions of years showing the names of major divisions and approximate times of the beginning and ending of the divisions. *Modified from Ross 1963.*

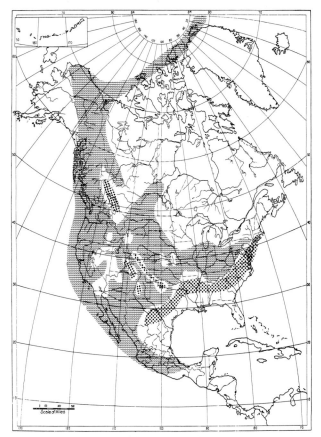

UPLAND MASS: dots; SEAS: wavy lines

FIG. 2.12. Approximate distribution of land area and seas on the proto–North American continent during the upper Pennsylvanian era. *Allen and Cox, unpublished manuscript.*

covered with water (or glacial ice). The presence of this landmass for some 310 million years is a significant fact when considering not only the history of the Ozarks, but also the history of North America as a whole.

At about the same time that the Ozarks were being uplifted, the Ouachita Mountains were also being formed. Unlike the Ozark uplift, the Ouachitas appear to be the result of an ancient southern continent ramming into the North American continental plate (fig. 2.12). When two continental plates collide, something has to give way; in this case, it was an extensive "ridge" of land across southwest Texas, southern Arkansas, northern Mississippi, Alabama, and Georgia. In effect, a high ridge was thrust upward.

The ridge connected the Ouachita Mountains with the eastern Appalachian Mountains (the Great Smoky Mountains of Tennessee and North Carolina) (fig. 2.12). To the west, the ridge eventually divided into the Arbuckle and Wichita Mountains in Oklahoma. This connection lasted for nearly 200 million years, but was severed during the early Cretaceous (fig. 2.13). The continuous east-west ridge was apparently broken by a

subsidence in eastern Arkansas and Mississippi and the opening of the Mississippi River valley. Again, this severance with eastern North America is a significant fact when one considers the origin and evolution of plants and animals in Arkansas and North America.

It is easy to tell whether you are in the Ozark or Ouachita Mountains without the aid of a map. In the Ozark Mountains the rocks are stacked on top of one another like a layered cake (fig. 2.14). In contrast, the rocks of the Ouachita Mountains are twisted and turned and the strata are directed almost vertically toward the sky (fig. 2.15). These upward projecting strata are the result of the tremendous forces that came to bear on the strata as the North American plate collided with a southern continent. Such forces as occurred in southern Arkansas some 300 million years ago would make the California earthquakes of recent times look rather puny in comparison.

Between the northern Ozarks and the southern Ouachitas is the Arkansas River valley, also known as the Arkhoma Basin. The Arkhoma Basin is geologically different from its southern and northern counterparts.

UPLAND MASS: dots; SEAS: wavy lines

FIG. 2.13. Approximate distribution of mountains and epicontinental seas during the upper Cretaceous. *Allen and Cox, unpublished manuscript.*

For one thing, the Arkhoma Basin is rich in gas and oil deposits and, to a lesser extent, in coal.

The Arkhoma Basin is also thought to have been uplifted during the Pennsylvanian. Once uplifted, the area was affected by the erosional forces of wind and water to a greater degree than the Ozark/Ouachita area. The erosion that occurred over much of the basin area left standing a series of large and small mountains. Three of the largest and most prominent features of the Arkhoma Basin are Petit Jean Mountain (fig. 2.16), near Morrilton, Mount Nebo, near Russellville, and Magazine Mountain, near Paris. These three mountains and many lesser mountains can be easily seen along Interstate 40.

The fossil record during the Triassic and Jurassic periods of the Mesozoic era is sparse, so it is difficult to tell what events were taking place in the Ozark/Ouachita area; however, we do know that most of North America was free of inland seas and the climate seems to have been tropical.

In the beginning of the Cretaceous, the epicontinental seas invaded North America, dividing the eastern and western parts of the continent and completely surrounding the Ozark/Ouachita uplift. Fossil dinosaur bones from several areas in Arkansas and fossil dinosaur tracks from near Hope in southwest Arkansas (fig. 2.17) attest to the fact that fauna and flora were flourishing. It was during the early or midddle part of the Cretaceous period that the ridge between eastern North America and the Ouachita Mountains was broken. Thus, one avenue of possible east-west transit for plants and animals ceased to exist.

FIG. 2.14. The stacked layers of the geological strata characteristic of the Ozark Mountains. *Photograph by Robert T. Allen.*

FIG. 2.15. The geological strata of the Ouachita are characteristically thrust upward. *Photograph by Robert T. Allen.*

FIG. 2.16. Petit Jean Mountain as seen from Interstate 40 near Morrilton. *Photograph by Robert T. Allen.*

FIG. 2.17. Dinosaur tracks found near Hope, Arkansas, provide evidence that these large creatures inhabited the state during the Cretaceous period. *Photograph by Robert T. Allen.*

During the latter part of the Cretaceous and continuing into the early Tertiary, the world was, in effect, taking on many of the characteristics we see today. The dinosaurs became extinct at the end of the Cretaceous, and mammals and flowering plants began to radiate throughout the Tertiary period into a myriad of different forms and spread throughout the world as climatic patterns changed and shifted. These events resulted in significant changes in the composition and distribution patterns of the world's biota.

Many of the families of plants and animals that we recognize today had evolved by the beginning of the last major geological period, the Tertiary. Midway through this period, in the Miocene, another dramatic change took place on the North American continent that directly affected the biota of Arkansas. The western Rocky Mountain region experienced a tremendous uplift. The front range of the Rocky Mountains was thrust upward reaching the lofty peaks that we see today (fig. 2.18). Prevailing winds from the west caused a rain shadow effect on the eastern side of the mountains and Arkansas became dryer.

Great forests that once extended across North America were not able to survive the aridness of the eastern front range of the Rocky Mountains. These forests receded eastward into the area they now occupy. The rain shadow created by the Rocky Mountain Orogeny allowed for the origin and development of a "new" natural area, the Grassland Biome, in what we call the Great Plains. Ungulates such as bison, antelope,and pronghorn soon filled the Great Plains. In

FIG. 2.18. Approximate distribution of major mountain systems and seas during the Miocene.

Arkansas the climate was dryer, but the mountain springs and streams and slightly cooler temperatures probably provided numerous isolated habitats in which moisture-seeking and cool-tolerant plants and animals could survive.

Glaciers were the last of the great cataclysms to affect North America. Giant ice sheets covered most of Canada and much of the northern United States only a few thousand years ago (fig. 2.19). These ice sheets came and went several times, causing many species to become displaced southward into what have been called refugia. From studies of existing species and their close relatives and present-day distributions, two prominent refugia have been recognized in eastern North America: the Great Smoky Mountains and the Ozark/Ouachita uplift areas. Many species found a safe haven in these areas until the ice sheets receded.

As the glaciers melted, some of the species moved northward to inhabit the recently freed land. In some instances, especially well documented in stonefly literature (Ross and Ricker 1971), populations were left behind as other populations migrated northward. The northern populations eventually became ecologically

and geographically isolated from their southern counterparts. The now-isolated populations changed independently of one another to such an extent that they are now recognized as two distinct species (see chap. 8).

It is obvious that Arkansas has had a dynamic, sometimes dramatic, history. The ebb and flow of organisms into and out of the area has afforded ample opportunities for time, nature, and change to work on plants and animals. Only during the past thirty years have we really begun to piece together the story of the natural history of Arkansas. One can only hope that our civilization's "progress" will leave enough natural areas for future generations to be able to fill in the large lacuna that now exists in our knowledge.

The Importance of Microhabitats

Microhabitats are special places within larger habitats that may provide just the right environmental conditions for a species to live. Microhabitats may be small in area, as in the case of an intermittent pool of water along a mountain stream, or they may cover a more extensive area, such as the narrow spaces between rocks on a hillside. Throughout time, microhabitats have no doubt been important in preserving many species as climates waxed and waned and glaciers came and went. Arkansas, especially the mountainous area, is a

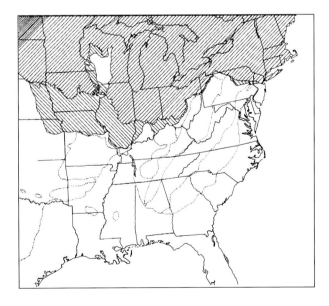

FIG. 2.19. Approximate location of glaciers on the North American continent during the Pleistocene era. *Redrawn from Ross 1965.*

particularly good area to observe microhabitats and some of their inhabitants.

Many of the species discussed in this book owe their survival to microhabitats. An example of such a species is the hay scented fern. This fern, which derives its common name from the fact that when its leaves are macerated they smell like freshly baled hay, has a distributional range predominantly in the northeastern part of the United States. In the Northeast the fern is common and even grows along roadsides. In the southern part of the range the plant becomes rare. In the Interior Highlands of Missouri and Arkansas there are only a few isolated populations. One such isolated population occurs on Magazine Mountain. On this mountain, hay scented fern clings to small crevices and indentations along the upper part of the cliff face. The crevices are just moist enough and cool enough to provide microhabitats for this fern species.

Another microhabitat inhabitant is the spinulose wood fern (*Dryopteris carthusiana* [Villars]). Peck (1986) reported the existence of a population of this fern living on Magazine Mountain near Brown Springs. Like hay scented fern, spinulose wood fern has a predominantly northeastern distribution. Besides the Magazine Mountain locality, the spinulose wood fern is also known to be located at the entrance of Rowland Cave in Stone County. These two Arkansas records represent the most extreme southwestern populations of this species. Of these isolated populations Peck (1986) said, "The occurrence of this northern species in Arkansas appears to be related to 'northern' environmental factors provided in Logan Co. by elevation (860 m) at the top of the tallest mountain in Arkansas and in Stone Co. by moderated, cool, moist air flowing from a cave entrance."

3

The Plants

There are approximately twenty-four hundred species of plants occurring in the state of Arkansas (Tucker 1974). All plants can be divided into two basic groups: vascular and nonvascular plants. Vascular plants have roots, stems, and leaves and include most Arkansas flora. Conversely, nonvascular plants have no roots, stems, or leaves and include algae, fungi, mosses, and liverworts. Both vascular and nonvascular plants can be further divided into two subdivisions. The nonvascular plants can be divided into thallophytes (algae and fungi) and bryophytes (mosses and liverworts), while the vascular plants can be divided into pteridophytes (ferns) and spermatophytes (seed-bearing plants). Seed-bearing plants can be further subdivided into gymnosperms (conifers) and angiosperms (flowering plants).

Within the angiosperm division there are monocotyledons and dicotyledons. Monocots usually have flower parts (sepals, petals, stamens, and pistils) in multiples of three and have parallel veins in their leaves. Familiar Arkansas monocot families include grasses (Gramineae), lillies (Liliaceae), irises (Iridaceae), orchids (Orchidaceae), and sedges (Cyperaceae). Dicots have flower parts in multiples of four or five, have veined leaves, and usually have fibrous roots. Most of the 2400 plant species in Arkansas are dicots.

Phylum Bryophyta— Mosses and Liverworts

The mosses and liverworts belong to the phylum Bryophyta, collectively termed the bryophytes. These primitive green plants lack conductive tissue and do not have true leaves, stems, or roots. In addition, bryophytes reproduce by spores and not true seeds.

Arkansas has a single endemic bryophyte, a leafy liverwort growing in Stone County (Paul Redfearn, pers. comm., 1989). Liverworts are divided into two groups based on growth form. They are either *thalloid*, meaning they grow flat against the surface as ribbons or scales, or they are *leafy* liverworts, which have stems, small rounded leaves, and often lateral branches.

Plagiochila japonica Sde. Lac. ex Miquel subspecies *ciliigera* Schuster 1959: 354

Liverwort

FIGURE 3.1

This is the only endemic liverwort of Arkansas (Paul Redfearn, pers. comm., 1989) and has been taken from only one area in Stone County, Arkansas. It grows in flat green patches over calcareous rocks. The leaves are thin, very delicate, and uniformly persistent. This

FIG. 3.1. Distribution of *Phagiochila japonica*.

subspecies possesses a shiny cuticle, and the leaves have distinctive narrow-based aciculate marginal teeth which are only one to three cells wide at the base and end in a filiform row of elongate cells formed of three to five or, rarely, six superimposed cells.

TYPE DEPOSITORY. R. L. McGregor 5413.
TYPE LOCALITY. Arkansas: Stone County; Big Sink Hole, Sylamore National Forest, Stone County. Collector: R. L. McGregor.
DISTRIBUTION. Known only from the type locality.

Spermatophyta— Seed Plants

Family Caryophyllaceae— Pink Family

Arenaria muriculata Maguire 1951: 507
Sandwort
FIGURE 3.2

This annual sandwort was described by the American botanist Bassett Maguire (1951) as a distinctive new member of the genus. Its small but prominent white flowers are produced in profusion and terminate the plant's slender stems during April–June. Maguire indicated it is, "Very similar and closely related to, and probably derived from *Arenaria patula*. Distinguished by its black muriculate-papillose seed, which in *A.*

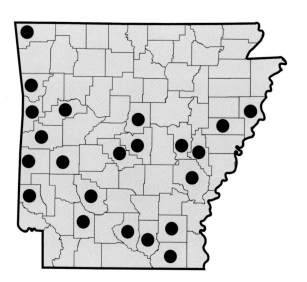

FIG. 3.2. Distribution of *Arenaria muriculata*.

patula are gray-brown and elongate-tuberculate, in *Arenaria* a most significant difference."

The habitat was described by Maguire (1951) as "prairies, meadows, rocky (limestone) glades and open woodland slopes." Maguire described it from six scattered Arkansas counties. Smith (1988) examined vouchers for twenty counties and indicated reports from four additional counties. The pattern of distribution suggests the species may occur also in surrounding states.

TYPE DEPOSITORY. Holotype: D. Demaree 14920, New York Botanical Garden. Date: 9 May 1937.
TYPE LOCALITY. Arkansas: Prairie County; Ulm, prairies, elev. 215 ft.
DISTRIBUTION. Arkansas: Arkansas, Ashley, Benton, Bradley, Calhoun, Clark, Crawford, Crittenden, Drew, Faulkner, Logan, Monroe, Montgomery, Nevada, Polk, Prairie, Pulaski, Saline, St. Francis, Scott, Sebastian, Sevier.

Family Cyperaceae—Sedge Family

Carex bicknellii var. opaca F. J. Hermann 1972: 49
Sedge
FIGURE 3.3

This taxon was described from the prairie region of east-central Arkansas by Hermann (1972) from three collections made by Dr. Delzie Demaree. Demaree found this plant on virgin prairies near Hazen and Ulm in the Grand Prairie region, an area in which almost all of the original prairie has been destroyed and converted to rice production.

Hermann's variety is separated from the typical variety by highly technical characters. Members of the genus *Carex* have their one-seeded fruits contained within inflated sacs called perigynia. Relative to their attachment to the inflorescence axis the perigynia show dorsal (upper) and ventral (lower) surfaces. The two varieties of the species are separated by subtle but significant differences in size, texture, prominence of venation, outline, and color of perigynia.

Smith (1988) said, "I am doubtful that it is a very useful variety, since it overlaps var. *Bicknellii* in size of the perigynia, and the Palmer specimen cited below . . . has the ventral; surface of the Perigynia rather clearly veined." On the other hand, Hermann is recognized worldwide as an authority on the genus *Carex*, and the var. *opaca* is recognized by most other specialists working in this highly complex genus of plants.

TYPE DEPOSITORY. Holotype: D. Demaree 60141, United States National Herbarium. Date: 10 May 1969.

FIG. 3.3. Distribution of *Carex bicknellii* var. *opaca*.

TYPE LOCALITY. Arkansas: Prairie County; Hazen, river terraces (never plowed), rice region.
DISTRIBUTION. Arkansas: Lonoke, Prairie.

Family Ranunculaceae— Buttercup Family

Delphinium newtonianum D. M. Moore 1939: 196

Moore's Delphinium

FIGURES 3.4, 3.5

This species was discovered by the late Dwight M. Moore, dean of Arkansas botanists, in 1935 in Newton County and named for his father (Newton Moore) and the county in which the new species occurred (Moore 1939). This lovely plant is about 2 feet high (60 cm) with flowers 1–1.25 inches (2.5–3 cm) long. Flowers usually are a sky blue color but darker colors occasionally occur and rarely white flowers are found. Flowering period is June to July.

This species of *Delphinium* is unusual among the American species of the genus, being our only species in which the flowers are arranged in open, branched inflorescences rather than the unbranched, elongate racemes common to other American species. The species is easily recognized by the long stalks on which one to several flowers are attached.

The habitat typically is in rich, moist upland woods. Most often the forest in which it is found has experienced high-grading timber practices at some point in the past. This Arkansas endemic has a

bicentric distribution in the state. In the Boston Mountains it is found locally in numerous sites in a four-county area and in two counties in the Ouachita Mountains.

TYPE DEPOSITORY. Holotype: D. M. Moore 350074, Missouri Botanical Garden (St. Louis). Date: 4 July 1935.
TYPE LOCALITY. Arkansas: Newton County; 2 mi. S of Jasper along old Hwy. 7.
DISTRIBUTION. Arkansas: Johnson, Montgomery, Newton, Pike, Pope, Searcy.

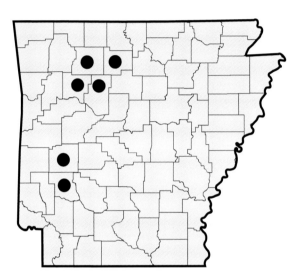

FIG. 3.4. Distribution of *Delphinium newtonianum*.

FIG. 3.5. *Delphinium newtonianum*, Moore's Delphinium, is found in only a few counties in the Ozark and Ouachita Mountains of Arkansas. *Photograph by Carl Hunter.*

Family Saxifragaceae—Saxifrage Family

Heuchera villosa Michx. var. *arkansana* (Rydberg) 1905: E. B. Smith 1977: 100

Arkansas Alumroot

FIGURES 3.6, 3.7

Arkansas alumroot was described as a species by the botanist Per Axel Rydberg in 1905, but it was reduced to varietal status by E. B. Smith (1977), a treatment followed also by the most recent monographer of the genus (Wells, 1984). Regardless of its taxonomic position the taxon is restricted to Arkansas.

The flowers of the endemic alumroot are small, white, and are in clusters on short stalks, while the leaves are rather large, attractive, and somewhat hairy (Hunter 1984). This species may be found in flower from July until the occurrence of killing frost in the fall. It is a perennial herb from a short rhizome, without a leafy stem and grows to about one foot or less in height.

Arkansas alumroot is a species of shaded bluffs, drainages, and seepage slopes, usually on sandstone substrates, in forested areas. The microhabitat may be in local forest openings, as on moist bluff faces or on rock boulders in a streambed, but the general habitat is in the shade of mixed hardwoods where a good moisture supply exists.

TYPE DEPOSITORY. Holotype: J. N. Blankenship s.n., Harvard University. Isotypes: New York Botanical Garden, University of Wisconsin. Date: 16 August 1895.
TYPE LOCALITY. Arkansas: Benton County; shady cliffs near Springdale. Nielsen and Younge (1938) believed

FIG. 3.7. *Heuchera villosa* var. *arkansana*, Arkansas Alumroot is known from a number of counties in Arkansas but appears to be confined to the state. *Photograph by Carl Hunter.*

the type locality was at Martin's Bluff, a large bluff on the Sylamore sandstone in southeast Benton County and extending into Washington County and now largely inundated by waters related to the reservoir impoundment at Beaver Lake.
DISTRIBUTION. Arkansas: Benton, Cleburne, Faulkner, Franklin, Johnson, Madison, Montgomery, Newton, Pope, Washington, Stone.

Family Rosaceae—Rose Family

Mespilus canescens Phipps 1990: 26

Stern's Medlar

FIGURES 3.8, 3.9

Recent critical reexamination of specimens housed in the University of Arkansas Herbarium rejected from the genus *Crataegus* resulted in the discovery of a new generic record for the North American flora, a totally new species described by Phipps (1990) and named *Mespilus canescens*. This new state endemic plant is an exceptionally beautiful multistemmed shrub or small tree, 5–7 m tall, with deciduous sage green leaves, flaking bark, and a scent like *Filipendula*, but lighter (Phipps 1990).

TYPE DEPOSITORY. Holotype: J. E. Stern, s.n., University of Arkansas Herbarium.
TYPE LOCALITY. Arkansas: Prairie County; 2 km S. of Slovak on the Konecny Grove Natural Area. Date: 15 April 1970. Collector: J. E. Stern.
DISTRIBUTION. Known only from the type locality.

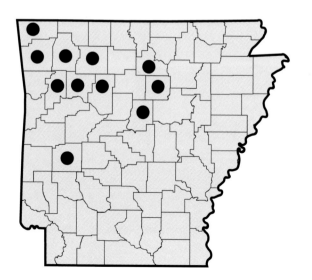

FIG. 3.6. Distribution of *Heuchera villosa* var. *arkansana*.

FIG. 3.8. Distribution of *Mespilus canescens* in Arkansas.

FIG. 3.9. Stern's medlar, *Mespilus canescens*, is one of the few Arkansas endemic plant species found in lowland areas in the state. *Photograph by Carl Hunter.*

Family Fagaceae—Beech Family

Quercus shumardi Buckl. var. *acerifolia* E. J. Palmer 1927: 737

Maple-Leaved Oak

FIGURES 3.10, 3.11

This diminutive oak was discovered on Magazine Mountain in 1924 by the botanist E. J. Palmer (Palmer 1927). Palmer at that time was retracing the path through Arkansas followed by the naturalist Thomas Nuttall on his noted trip into Arkansas Territory in 1819 (Nuttall 1821). The maple-leaved oak has three to five unusually broad lobed leaves, the palmate outlines

of which superficially resemble those of a maple. Typically it is a shrub or small tree, three to nine meters tall. Rarely it has a single trunk, but more often it consists of a group of several stems. Its acorns are smaller than other upland red oaks; the nut, when removed from the cap, is seldom more than twelve millimeters in length.

Much controversy surrounds this taxon. Some authorities feel it should be maintained as a good variety, while others (Smith 1988) feel it should be reduced to synonymy with typical *Q. shumardi*. Mohlenbrock (1985) suggested it may merit recognition at the species level, a view supported by William Hess (1989). Dr. Hess has studied the maple-leaved oak extensively over a three-year period and believes it is distinctive from all other variants of *Q. shumardi* he has seen. The late Delzie Demaree often related the story that Palmer had told him he was not sure the maple-leaved oak's relationships were with Shumard oak, but he was reluctant to describe it as a new species from a single site and didn't know what else to do with it.

This plant retains its distinctive leaf outlines, small acorns, and diminutive habit when cultivated at other locations. The foilage turns a brilliant red in early autumn, a character which distinguishes it from other members of the Shumard oak complex.

It is found in open woods at the edges of cliffs and on upper slopes on top of Magazine Mountain.

TYPE DEPOSITORY. Holotype: E. J. Palmer 26434, Arnold Arboretum (Harvard University). Date: 8 October 1924.
TYPE LOCALITY. Arkansas: Logan County; Magazine Mountain, Brown Springs.
DISTRIBUTION. Known only from the type locality.

FIG. 3.10. Distribution of *Quercus shumardii* var. *acerifolia.*

FIG. 3.11. *Quercus shumardi* var. *acerifolia*, the maple-leaved oak is found only on Magazine Mountain in Arkansas. This tree variety is a curious biological phenomenon whose origin is a mystery. *Photograph by Carl Hunter.*

Order Solanales

Family Hydrophyllaceae— Waterleaf Family

Hydrophyllum brownei Kral and Bates 1991: 60

Browne's Waterleaf

FIGURE 3.12, 3.13

Although first collected by George Engelmann in 1837, this species was not formally recognized and described as new until 1991, when Kral and Bates (1991) reviewed new material collected by Vernon Bates and compared that with earlier specimens from the Ouachita Mountains of Arkansas. Currently, this new species is the only member of its genus known to occur in the Ouachita Mountains. Browne's waterleaf is a mesic-woodland perennial that grows in silt loams or loams with a variable sand or clay fraction. It can also be found in talus of rich, shaded slopes or in the rocky, better drained terraces along Ouachita Mountain streams. Typically found under a deciduous forest of oak, elm, hackberry, maple, hickory, and ash, Browne's waterleaf is frequently associated with other herbs such as windflower, bloodroot, wild geranium, wild ginger, sweet cicely, Jacob's ladder, toothwort, and various violets and sedges. The primary leaves are basally

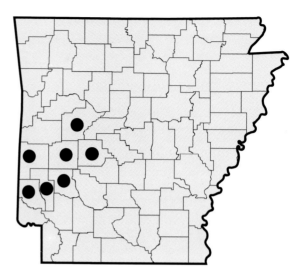

FIG. 3.12. Distribution of *Hydrophyllum brownei*.

disposed, while the flowers are located in one or two clusters at the top of a long, leafless stalk (peduncle). The leaves are very dissected and quite hairy, 1–4 dm long. The peduncle, about 2–3 mm thick and 2–4 dm high, is also noticeably hairy. The attractive white or lavender flowers appear by May 1 and quickly fade by May 15. The mature fruits are oval-shaped capsules, about 3-3.5 mm, containing a few brownish colored seeds. Perhaps the most striking feature of this waterleaf is its adaptation to rocky detritus by the formation of long, whiplike, tuber-forming rhizomes that may exceed 1 m in length.

TYPE DEPOSITORY. Holotype: R. Kral and V. Bates 76352, Missouri Botanical Garden.
TYPE LOCALITY. Arkansas: Polk County; terraces and silty bottoms along Big Fork Creek at Opal, about 3 mi.

FIG. 3.13. *Hydrophyllum brownei*. *Photograph by Vernon Bates.*

N. of Hwy. 8 and Big Fork (T2S, R28W, Sec. 28, SE1/4). Date: 22 May 1989. Collectors: R. Kral and V. Bates.
DISTRIBUTION. Arkansas: Garland, Howard, Montgomery, Pike, Polk, Sevier, Yell.

Order Papaverales

Family Cruciferae—Mustard Family

Cardamine angustata var. *ouachitana* E. B. Smith 1982: 379

Toothwort

FIGURE 3.14

Smith (1982) recognized and described this new variety of toothwort endemic to the Ouachita Mountains of

western Arkansas differentiating it from *Cardamine angustata* var. *angustata* in having the leaf margins consistently and absolutely glabrous. This early spring–flowering herbaceous perennial had been collected repeatedly in the Ouachita Mountains over the last three decades.

TYPE DEPOSITORY. Holotype: E. B. Smith 3664, University of Arkansas Herbarium.
TYPE LOCALITY. Arkansas: Polk County; common along the Cossatot River, 12.1 mi. S. of the junction of Hwys. 375 and 8 near Mena. Date: 19 March 1985. Collector: E. B. Smith
DISTRIBUTION. Arkansas: Howard, Montgomery, Polk.

Order Rubiales

Family Rubiaceae—Madder Family

Galium arkansasum var. *pubiflorum* E. B. Smith 1979: 281

FIGURE 3.15

Galium arkansanum, a small herbaceous perennial with leaves in whorls of four, is endemic to the Ozark and Ouachita mountains of Oklahoma, Arkansas, and Missouri (Steyermark 1963, Smith 1979). Smith (1979) compared Oklahoma and Arkansas populations of *G. arkansanum* morphologically and determined that specimens from Montgomery County had longer hairs (0.7–1.3 mm) on the underside of the corolla lobes. Because this "pure" hairy corolla material was limited to Montgomery County with mixtures of this condition in other areas, Smith (1979) suggested that this new phase be treated as a new variety.

TYPE DEPOSITORY. Holotype: E. B. Smith 3358, University of Arkansas Herbarium.
TYPE LOCALITY. Arkansas: Montgomery County; scattered at the edge of the dirt road to Albert Pike rec. area, 1.3 mi. S. of Hwy. 8. Date: 31 May 1978. Collector: E. B. Smith.
DISTRIBUTION. Known only from the type locality.

FIG. 3.15. Distribution of *Galium arkansanum* var. *pubiflorum*.

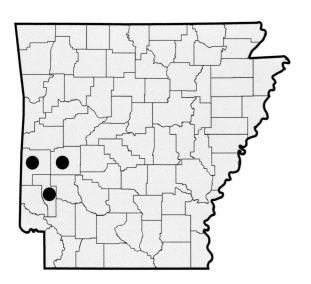

FIG. 3.14. Distribution of *Cardamine angustata* var. *ouachitana*.

Family Asteraceae— Composite Family

Polymnia cossatotensis A. B. Pittman and V. Bates 1990: 481

Cossatot Leafcup

FIGURES 3.16, 3.17, 3.18

This species was discovered in 1988 by Bert Pittman, an Arkansas Natural Heritage Commission botanist, and Vernon Bates, a freelance botanist doing contract research directed toward a botanical inventory of the Ouachita National Forest (Pittman, Bates, and Kral 1989). Despite an intensive search in nearby areas, the species is still known only from the type locality.

Polymnia cossatotensis is distinguished from other species in the genus by its annual habitat, cauline leaves with cordate bases, smaller number of ray flowers, and fruits of a larger size.

The habitat at the type locality is an open, unshaded area on novaculite talus.

TYPE DEPOSITORY. Holotype: Pittman and Bates 7222, Gray Herbarium, Harvard University. Date: 6 October 1988.

TYPE LOCALITY. Arkansas: Montgomery County; cherty novaculite talus along the Little Missouri River, east-facing side of Blaylock Mtn.

DISTRIBUTION. Known only from the type locality.

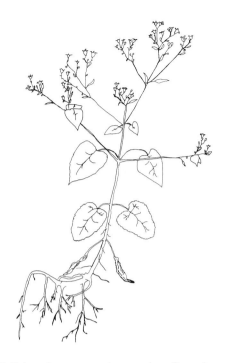

FIG. 3.17. *Polymnia cossatotensis*, general configuration and habitus of the species. *Redrawn from Pittman et al. 1989.*

FIG. 3.18. *Polymnia cossatotensis* is one of the most recently discovered and described plant species endemic to Arkansas. *Photograph by Vernon Bates.*

FIG. 3.16. Distribution of *Polymnia cossatotensis*.

4

Phylum Annelida

Segmented Worms

Segmented worms belong to the phylum Annelida, a large group of worms numbering around nine thousand species worldwide. This group contains the familiar earthworms and freshwater worms (oligochaetes) and leeches; however, most annelids are marine worms (polychaetes), which are less familiar to most people.

No one is sure of the number of annelid worms inhabiting Arkansas. At least two species, *Diplocardia meansi* and *Diplocardia sylvicola,* appear to be endemic to Rich Mountain in Polk County, Arkansas. Further intensive collecting throughout the Cossatot, Caddo, and Ozark Mountains may reveal additional endemic annelid worms.

Order Oligochaeta

Oligochaetes include a group of segmented worms numbering over three thousand species. Although they are commonly referred to as earthworms, many species inhabit freshwater, brackish, or marine waters, and some species are even parasitic. These "earthworms" bear setae (needlelike chitinous structures of the integument), which aid in locomotion of the species.

Diplocardia meansi Gates 1977:13
Earthworm

FIGURES 4.1, 4.2

Diplocardia meansi is the second largest known earthworm in the United States and occurs only on Rich Mountain in Polk County. It was discovered by Dr. Bruce Means on 11 June 1973 as he dug for salamanders on Rich Mountain. It was later named by Gates (1977).

This fascinating earthworm has been studied peri-

odically by Dr. Means for over twenty years. Several interesting aspects of the behavior and ecology of *D. meansi* have been communicated to us by Dr. Means (pers. comm. 1988). *D. meansi* is bioluminescent. If the species is tweaked or shocked in the dark, the glutinous and distasteful coelomic fluid it secretes will glow brightly. This earthworm lays cocoons with only one or two immatures in them.

D. meansi inhabits the drier soils of Rich Mountain, not the mesic and saturated soils along stream courses or seepage areas. On rainy nights in May this species migrates in large numbers (possibly to breed). Specimens have been picked up crossing the highway at night on Rich Mountain.

Gates (1977) reported the habitat as being located under and between large rocks imbedded in poorly developed soils (talus origin) of steep hillsides.

FIG. 4.1. Distribution of *Diplocardia meansi.*

TYPE DEPOSITORY. Unknown.

TYPE LOCALITY. Arkansas: Polk County; southern rock talus slope of Rich Mtn., 3 mi. W of Mena, elev. 2200 ft. Date: 11 June 1973. Collectors: D. B. Means (DBM-1847) and J. B. Atkinson.

DISTRIBUTION. Known only from the type locality.

FIG. 4.2. *Diplocardia meansi* is the second longest worm found in North America. When these worms are migrating and crossing roads in May, they are a spectacular phenomenon. *Photograph by D. B. Means.*

Diplocardia sylvicola Gates 1977: 14

Earthworm

FIGURE 4.3

The earthworm, *Diplocardia sylvicola,* differs from *D. meansi* by the saddle-shaped clitellum, slightly fewer segments (198–249), and smaller size (58–98 mm). It is also more widely distributed within the state than *D. meansi.*

TYPE DEPOSITORY. Unknown.
TYPE LOCALITY. Unknown.
DISTRIBUTION. Arkansas: Dallas, Garland, Polk.

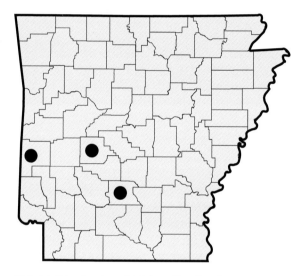

FIG. 4.3. Distribution of *Diplocardia sylvicola.*

5

Phylum Mollusca

Molluscs

The phylum Mollusca is a diverse group containing nearly 50,000 living species and over 35,000 fossil species. It is characterized by a soft body and an external calcareous shell. The phylum contains snails, slugs, mussels, clams, oysters, squids, and octopuses among others. Molluscs in Arkansas include snails, slugs, mussels, and clams. M. E. Gordon (1980) reported a total of 223 taxa of mollusca known from the state at that time. Of this total, 107 terrestrial gastropods, 36 aquatic gastropods, 65 unionoid mussels, and 15 sphaeriod clams made up the molluscan fauna of Arkansas. Recent research indicates a slightly more diverse fauna.

Class Gastropoda— Snails and Slugs

The class Gastropoda is the largest and most successful group of molluscs, containing approximately 35,000 living and 15,000 fossil species. Although there are snails without shells (slugs), most species in Arkansas have the body covered by a single shell which is usually coiled. Depending on the direction of the coil, snail shells may be said to be dextral (right handed) or sinistral (left handed); dextral shells are the most common. The mouth of the snail consists of an upper jaw, which holds food in place, and a specially toothed, tongue-like structure called a radula, which rasps off small bits of food. Locomotion is by way of a flat muscular structure called a "foot."

Snails in Arkansas are generally divided into two main groups based on respiration strategies: the Prosobranchia use a gill for respiration and the Pulmonata use a lung to obtain oxygen directly from

the air. Both land and aquatic snails occur in each group; however, most terrestrial snails are members of the Pulmonata.

As of 1986, 143 species of gastropods (107 terrestrial and 36 aquatic) were known from Arkansas. A total of 9 species of snails (5 terrestrial and 4 aquatic) are considered endemic to the state.

Family Hydrobiidae

Somatogyrus amnicoloides Walker 1915: 39
Ouachita Pebblesnail
FIGURES 5.1, 5.2

S. amnicoloides is about the size and shape of an *Amnicola*, as suggested by the specific name (Walker 1915). Mark Gordon (pers. comm. 1990) feels this

FIG 5.1. Distribution of *Somatogyrus amnicoloides*.

species is probably extinct, as recent collecting for it has proved futile. Its demise may be due to pollution or conditions caused by reservoir discharges.

The shell is small (about 2.75 mm in diameter), subglobose, rather thin, pale horn color, and smooth with very fine lines of growth. The outer lip is distinctly thickened in a projecting, broadly rounded angle at the meeting of the columella.

TYPE DEPOSITORY. Holotype: USNM 40012, United States National Museum, Bryant Walker Collection.
TYPE LOCALITY. Arkansas: Clark County; Ouachita River at Arkadelphia. Collector: H. E. Wheeler.
DISTRIBUTION. Known only from the type locality.

FIG. 5.2. General shape of the *Somatogyrus amnicoloides* shell. *Redrawn from Walker 1915.*

Somatogyrus crassilabris Walker 1915: 40

Thicklipped Pebblesnail

FIGURES 5.3, 5.4

S. crassilabris was taken only from the rocks on muddy banks of the North Fork of the White River in Baxter County. This species is probably extinct due to the destruction of the habitat by reservoirs and hypolimnetic releases (Mark Gordon, pers. comm.

FIG. 5.3. Distribution of *Somatogyrus crassilabris.*

1990). The shell is small (4 mm in diameter), subglobose, very thick and solid, greenish in color, and smooth with very fine lines of growth (Walker 1915). There are about four whorls, and the opiral whorl is small, rounded, and constricted by a rather deep suture. The aperature periphery is greatly thickened.

"This species, though evidently related to *S. wheeleri* Walker by reason of its shouldered body-whorl, differs decidedly in the characters of the apical whorls, the less pronounced shouldering of the body-whorl, the smaller umbilicus, and especially, in the remarkable thickening of the aperature" (Walker 1915).

TYPE DEPOSITORY. USNM 271763, United States National Museum.
TYPE LOCALITY. Arkansas: Baxter County; North Fork of White River near Norfolk. Collector: A. A. Hinkley.
DISTRIBUTION. Known only from the type locality.

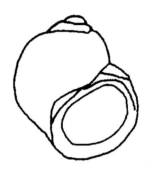

FIG. 5.4. General shape of the *Somatogyrus crassilabris* shell. *Redrawn from Walker 1915.*

Somatogyrus wheeleri Walker 1915: 51

Channelled Pebblesnail

FIGURES 5.5, 5.6

The aquatic snail, *Somatogyrus wheeleri*, is known only from the type locality. Mark Gordon (pers. comm. 1990) feels this species is also extinct due to environmental alteration caused by reservoirs and hypolimnetic releases. (See *S. anmicoloides.*)

TYPE DEPOSITORY. Holotype: USNM 33900, United States National Museum of Natural History, Bryant Walker Collection.
TYPE LOCALITY. Arkansas: Clark County; Ouachita River at Arkadelphia. Collector: H. E. Wheeler.
DISTRIBUTION. Known only from the type locality.

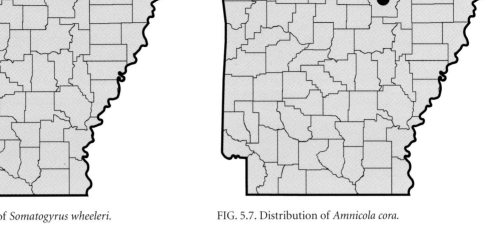

FIG. 5.5. Distribution of *Somatogyrus wheeleri*.

FIG. 5.7. Distribution of *Amnicola cora*.

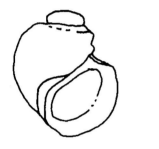

FIG. 5.6. General shape of the *Somatogyrus wheeleri* shell. *Redrawn from Walker 1915.*

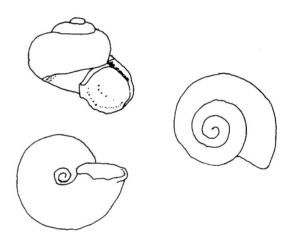

FIG. 5.8. General morphology and shape of the *Amnicola cora*. *Redrawn from Hubricht 1979.*

Amnicola cora Hubricht 1979: 142

Foushee Cavesnail

FIGURES 5.7, 5.8

Amnicola cora is apparently a true troglobitic species that lives in cave streams in Independence County. This small, pale yellow aquatic snail has a shape about 1.6 mm in height and 2.0 mm in diameter and has about 3.3 whorls. It is blind with no trace of eyes (Hubricht 1979). *A. cora* is most closely related to *A. stygis* Hubricht, a troglobitic species found in Perry County, Missouri.

TYPE DEPOSITORY. Holotype: FMNH 193762, Field Museum of Natural History.
TYPE LOCALITY. Arkansas: Independence County; Foushee Cave, 3 mi. W of Locust Grove. Collectors: N. and J. Youngsteadt and L. Hubricht.
DISTRIBUTION. Known only from the type locality.

Family Zonitidae

Paravitrea aulacogyra (Pilsbry and Ferriss) 1906: 561

Mount Magazine Supercoil

FIGURES 5.9, 5.10

The holotype for this specimen was perfect when found, although it was bleached. It is the sole specimen collected of this species. Pilsbry (1940) later wrote, "this shell was broken near the mouth by someone using it, since it was described and drawn in 1906, so that no entire specimen is now known to exist in collections."

The single shell is 8 mm wide and 3.3 mm high with 5.5 whorls. Pilsbry (1940) commented that *P. aulacogyra* is closely related to *P. petrophila*.

Leslie Hubricht speculates this may be the young of some other species (H. W. Robison, pers. comm. 1984).

TYPE DEPOSITORY. Holotype: ANSP 91334, Academy of Natural Sciences of Philadelphia.

TYPE LOCALITY. Arkansas: Logan County; Magazine Mountain in talus on north side of summit, elev. about 2800 ft. Collector: H. A. Pilsbry.

DISTRIBUTION. Known only from the type locality.

FIG. 5.9. Distribution of *Paravitrea aulacogyra.*

Family Polygyridae

Polygyra peregrina Rehder 1932: 130
White Liptooth

FIGURES 5.11, 5.12

This small snail is 8 mm wide and 4.5 mm high and inhabits rock cliffs in the Ozark Mountains of northern Arkansas. It is a glossy, generally pale-colored snail with about 6–6.25 whorls. The parietal tooth in *P. peregrina* is pointed and prominent, while the basal tooth is farther out on the lip.

TYPE DEPOSITORY. Holotype: MCZ 81349, Museum of Comparative Zoology, Harvard University.

TYPE LOCALITY. Arkansas: Izard County; foot of White River's dolomite bluffs at Calico Rock. Collector: Ernest J. Palmer.

DISTRIBUTION. Arkansas: Izard, Marion, Newton, Searcy, Stone

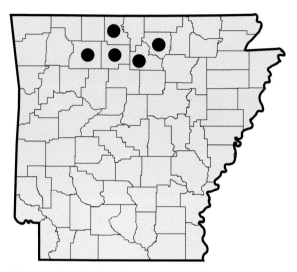

FIG. 5.11. Distribution of *Polygyra peregrina.*

FIG. 5.12. General shape of *Polygyra peregrina. Redrawn from Rehder 1932.*

Mesodon clenchi (Rehder) 1932: 129
Calico Rock Oval

FIGURES 5.13, 5.14

The Calico Rock oval was described from specimens collected by the famous botanist Ernest J. Palmer at the

FIG. 5.10. General morphology and shape of *Paravitrea aulacogyra. Redrawn from Pilsbry and Ferriss 1906.*

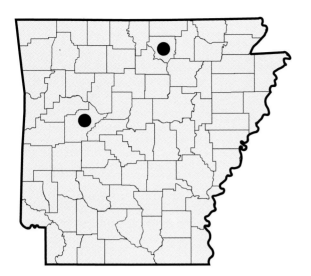

FIG. 5.13. Distribution of *Mesodon clenchi.*

Mesodon magazinensis (Pilsbry and Ferriss) 1906: 545

Magazine Mountain Shagreen

FIGURES 5.15, 5.16

The Magazine Mountain shagreen snail lives on rock slides under a cliff on the north slope of Magazine Mountain at an elevation of about 2800 feet. This dusky brown to buff-colored land snail is about 0.5 inches (13 mm) wide and 0.3 inches (7 mm) high. The shell has five whorls (Pilsbry and Ferriss 1906) and is similar to *Mesodon inflectus* (Say), except that it is more abruptly contracted behind the lip, and the crest preceding the contraction, above periphery, is more prominent (Pilsbry 1940). The aperture is bluntly triangular with the outer lip having a small conic tooth. In the basal lip, instead of a tooth there is a low swelling near the columella. There are scalelike periostracal processes well developed.

On 17 April 1989, this snail was officially declared a federally threatened species under the Endangered Species Act.

foot of White River's dolomite bluffs at Calico Rock in Izard County. Leslie Hubricht found specimens living under ledges and edges of a rock slide. On Mount Nebo, he found several dead shells around the edge of a rock slide. Hubricht reported, "One would probably have to go out at night after a rain to find living ones" (pers. comm. 1984)

Characteristically, this dark straw-colored species has a dull luster and a rather solid depressed shell. The upper surface is flattened and has about five whorls; the last whorl is rounded at the periphery. The sculpture consists of low irregular striations and minute irregular spiral lines (Rehder 1932). The aperture is subcircular and slightly oblique. The peristome is white and thickened. This snail is about 20–22 mm wide and about 17–18 mm high.

TYPE DEPOSITORY. Holotype: MCZ 81347, Museum of Comparative Zoology, Harvard University.
TYPE LOCALITY. Arkansas: Izard County; White River bluffs, 1 mi. below Calico Rock. Collector: Ernest J. Palmer.
DISTRIBUTION. Arkansas: Izard, Yell.

FIG. 5.15. Distribution of *Mesodon magazinensis.*

FIG. 5.14. General morphology and shape of *Mesodon clenchi. Redrawn from Rehder 1932.*

FIG. 5.16. General morphology and shape of *Mesodon magazinensis*. Redrawn from Pilsbry and Ferriss 1906.

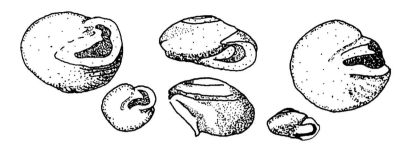

TYPE DEPOSITORY. Holotype: ANSP 91314, Academy of Natural Sciences of Philadelphia.

TYPE LOCALITY. Arkansas: Logan County; Magazine Mountain. Collectors: H. A. Pilsbry and J. H. Ferriss. Date: 28–30 March 1903.

DISTRIBUTION. Known only from the type locality.

Class Bivalvia— Mussels and Clams

The Class Bivalvia (Pelycepoda in older publications) is characterized by a bivalved shell and the presence of a muscular "foot." In addition, mussels and clams have no radula for feeding and exhibit little cephalization.

In Arkansas, sixty-five species of unionoid mussels and fifteen species of sphaerioid clams were listed by Gordon (1980) for the state; however, several other species have been found in the state since then. Of these, only three mussels, *Lampsilis powellii* (Lea), *Lampsilis streckeri* Frierson, and *Villosa arkansasensis* (Lea) are endemic to state waters.

Lampsilis powellii (Lea) 1852: 270

Arkansas Fatmucket

FIGURES 5.17, 5.18

Lampsilis powellii is a rare and, until recently, little-known freshwater mussel restricted to the Ouachita Mountains of western Arkansas. Reported collections of *L. powellii* from the Spring and Neosho Rivers in Oklahoma and Kansas and from the Black River in Missouri are misidentifications (Gordon and Harris 1985). Recent fieldwork has shown the mussel to occur in the upper portions of the Saline and Ouachita Rivers as well as the Caddo River, with stable populations present in the South Fork of the Ouachita River and the South Fork of the Saline River (Harris and Gordon 1987).

Unfortunately, a considerably large area of habitat

has been inundated by recent impoundments, which periodically utilize hypolimnetic discharge and thus jeopardize populations below these dams (Gordon and Harris 1985). Gordon and Harris (1985) suggested that due to the impoundments and the restricted range of

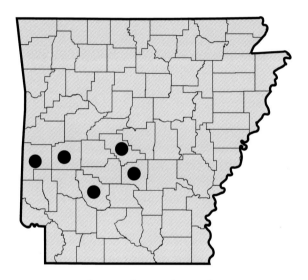

FIG. 5.17. Distribution of *Lampsilis powellii*

FIG. 5.18. *Lampsilis powellii* is confined to a few rivers in the Ouachita Mountains of Arkansas. *Photograph by Keith Sutton.*

L. powellii, some protected status appears warranted to ensure the survival of this species. Currently, the U.S. Fish and Wildlife Service is proposing to list *L. powellii* as a threatened species. Threats to the continued existence of this species include impoundments, channel alteration, gravel dredging, sedimentation, and the degradation of water quality.

The shell of the Arkansas fatmucket is generally of medium size, but occasionally exceeds 100 mm in length. It is elliptical to long obovate with subinflated valves. The umbos are moderately full and project slightly above the hinge line. Generally, the surface of the shell is smooth with a shiny olive brown to tawny periostracum, and it lacks rays. The nacre is bluish white and irridescent. Shells are sexually dimorphic (Johnson 1980).

Habitats preferred by *L. powellii* include deep pools and backwater areas with sand, sand gravel, sand-cobble, or sand-rock substrates with some current to remove organic debris. Although the fatmucket may be found near ripples, it is not found in areas of strong current and is not tolerant of impounded conditions.

TYPE DEPOSITORY. Holotype: USNM 85042, United States National Museum.
TYPE LOCALITY. Arkansas: Saline County; Saline River at Benton.
DISTRIBUTION. Arkansas: Clark, Grant, Montgomery, Polk, Saline.

Lampsilis streckeri Frierson 1927: 74

Speckled Pocketbook

FIGURES 5.19, 5.20

The speckled pocketbook is a federally endangered species. Harris and Gordon (1987) consider this mussel species to be endemic to Arkansas. It occurs only in the Little Red River system, with recent collections available from several localities in the upper Little Red River. This species is quite similar to *Lampsilis reeveiana* (Lea), a common species of the White River system (Gordon and Kraemer 1984). The relationship of these two species requires additional study. It is threatened by its limited range and low population levels. Reservoir construction, water pollution and channel modification have combined to eliminate *L. streckeri* from most of its historical range.

The speckled pocketbook has a thin shell 80 mm in length that is elliptical, dark yellow or brown with an overcast that is often green, and chevron spots that form rays in a chainlike arrangement. A sexually

dimorphic species, females may be broader and more evenly rounded posteriorly.

L. streckeri inhabits coarse to muddy sand in depths of up to 0.4 m (1.3 ft.) in flowing water.

TYPE DEPOSITORY. Holotype: UMMZ 875789, Museum of Zoology, University of Michigan.
TYPE LOCALITY. Arkansas: Van Buren County; Little Red River at Clinton.
DISTRIBUTION. Arkansas: Stone, Van Buren.

FIG. 5.19. Distribution of *Lampsilis streckeri.*

FIG. 5.20. *Lampsilis streckeri* is a rare mussel species listed as a federally endangered species. It occurs only in two counties in the Ozark Mountains of Arkansas. *Photograph by Keith Sutton.*

Villosa arkansasensis (Lea) 1862: 263

Ouachita Creekshell

FIGURES 5.21

This small mussel is typically found in small- to medium-sized streams in the Ouachita Mountains. It is a little-known species, not so much from its rarity as from the lack of surveys of streams which it inhabits. *Villosa arkansasensis* is generally associated with riffles but may be found in some pool situations. It is not tolerant of impoundments.

The *V. arkansasensis* is a small species with a shell usually not exceeding 40–50 mm. Despite its small size and relatively thin shell, the hinge teeth, particularly the anterior ones (pseudocardinals), are heavy. The periostracum is yellowish, greenish, or brownish in color and may have some narrow wavy rays that are usually most prevalent on the posterior portion of the shell. This species is sexually dimorphic, with the female a bit more swollen and broader than the males. Also, female shells often exhibit an indentation of the lower posterior margin. The *V. arkansasensis* may be confused with small specimens of *Obovaria jacksoniana* Frierson.

TYPE DEPOSITORY. USNM 25710, United States National Museum.

TYPE LOCALITY. Arkansas: Garland County; Ouachita River near Hot Springs.

DISTRIBUTION. Arkansas: Garland, Polk, Montgomery, Clark, Pike, Howard, Saline.

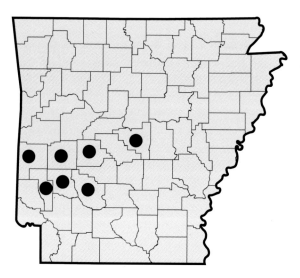

FIG. 5.21. Distribution of *Villosa arkansasensis.*

6

Subphylum Crustacea

Crustaceans

Recently, crustaceans have been elevated from a class to a subphylum level (Hickman et al. 1988). This group contains lobsters, crayfishes, isopods, amphipods, shrimp, crabs, copepods, barnacles, and others. The single true distinguishing characteristic of the crustaceans is the presence of two pairs of antennae. In addition, crustaceans usually have two pairs of maxillae on the head, a pair of mandibles, and a pair of appendages on each body segment. Gills may also be present.

Henry Robison (unpubl. studies) is currently studying the crustacean fauna of Arkansas.

Class Amphipoda— Amphipods

Although basically a marine group of crustaceans, amphipods number about eight hundred freshwater species worldwide; about ninety American species have been described (Pennak 1978). Characteristically, the body of an amphipod is compressed laterally, with seven thoracic segments, a six-segmented abdomen, and a small, terminal telson. Because of their habit of rolling over on their back or side when swimming, amphipods are often called "sideswimmers." Amphipods are often mistaken for freshwater shrimp; however, the two are only distantly related.

Only two of the thirteen species of amphipods known in the state are endemic. Each endemic is localized on a mountain, one occuring only on Rich Mountain and the other on the state's highest peak, Magazine Mountain.

Stygobromus elatus (Holsinger) 1967: 85

Magazine Mountain Amphipod

FIGURES 6.1, 6.2

Stygobromus elatus was collected from Magazine Mountain by Leslie Hubricht during his travels through Arkansas in 1940; however, this amphipod was not officially described until 1967 by Holsinger. Although closely related to *S. alabamensis* and *S. montanus*, *S. elatus* may be distinguished from *S. montanus* by having several slender ventral spines on the peduncular segment four of the second antenna, a straight propod palmar margin of gnathopod one, a slightly convex propod palmar margin of gnathopod two, a larger number of spine teeth on the palms of both gnathostomal propods, a proportionately shorter outer ramus of uropod two, a less elongate telson of the male, and a more apically spinose telson of the female.

FIG. 6.1. Distribution of *Stygobromus elatus.*

Nothing is known of the biology of this species, which has been collected from seeps on top of Magazine Mountain, the highest point in Arkansas coming from Pennsylvanian age sandstones (2,823 ft. [853 m] above sea level).

TYPE DEPOSITORY. Holotype: United States National Museum.
TYPE LOCALITY. Arkansas: Logan County; a seep on Magazine Mountain 0.2 mi. E of The Lodge. Collector: Leslie Hubricht. Date: 4 May 1940.
DISTRIBUTION. Known only from the type locality.

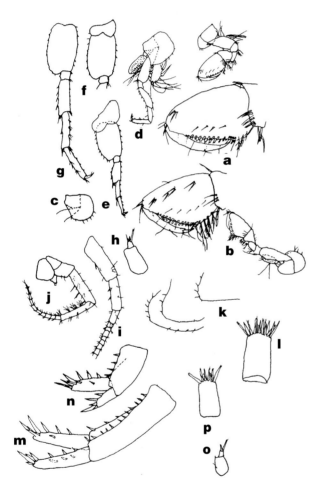

FIG. 6.2. *Stygobromus elatus*, female (9 mm): a, b, gnathopods 1, 2; c, coxal plate of pereiopod 3; d–g, pereiopods 4–7; h, uropod 3; i, j, antennae 1, 2; k, abdominal side plates; l, telson; m, n, uropods 1, 2. Male allotype (6 mm)(same locality): o, uropod 3; p, telson. *Redrawn from Holsinger 1967.*

Stygobromus montanus (Holsinger) 1967: 83
Rich Mountain Amphipod
FIGURES 6.3, 6.4

Holsinger (1967) described this Rich Mountain endemic from specimens collected previously by Leslie Hubricht and referred to by Hubricht and Mackin (1940) as "a distinctive lot," although they failed to recognize this material as a separate species. This amphipod is most closely related to *Stygobromus alabamensis;* however, it can be distinguished by the less concave and more spinose propod palmar margins of the gnathopods, the two spines (three in the female) on the ramus of the uropod, and more elongate and apical spines on the telson .

S. montanus is considered a member of the *tenuis* group, one of three major lines of evolution of the genus *Stygobromus* (Holsinger 1967). Ancestral stock of this group was presumably a widely distributed brackish-water form which inhabited coastal areas during the Mississippian embayment. *S. alabamensis* with its rather unspecialized morphology and wide range suggest it is not much different from the hypothetical ancestral form. During periods of Ozark peneplanation, it is suggested that wide dispersal of populations of *alabamensis* stock occurred. This could have come as late as the late Tertiary. The height of dispersal probably occurred by the early Quaternary with events throughout the Pleistocene, such as the general downcutting of land forms in the Ozark region,

FIG. 6.3. Distribution of *Stygobromus montanus.*

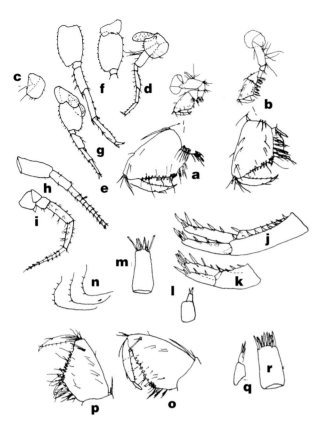

FIG. 6.4. *Stygobromus montanus*, male (8.25 mm): a, b, gnathopods 1, 2; c, coxal plate of pereiopod 3; d–g, pereiopod 4, 5, 6, 7;
h, i, antennae 1, 2; j–l, uropods 1, 2, 3; m, telson; n, abdominal
side plates. Female (9.00 mm) (same locality): o, p, gnathopods
1, 2; q, uropod 3; r, telson. *Redrawn from Holsinger 1967.*

causing local and regional isolation of stocks (e.g., *S.
montanus* on Rich Mountain and *S. elatus* on Magazine
Mountain).

Holsinger (1967) suggested that *S. montanus* is
restricted today to groundwater biotypes in the
Ouachita Mountains, whereas the range of the
alabamensis stock once extended into the Ouachitas.
He also suggested that extensive downcutting of this
area by stream erosion since the late Tertiary has
resulted in extrinsic barriers between populations of
this region and those farther north (e.g., Magazine
Mountain).

The largest record of a female is 9 mm and the
record for a male is 13 mm long (Holsinger, pers.
comm. 1981). Except for this brief information,
virtually nothing is known about its biology,
distribution, and ecology.

TYPE DEPOSITORY. Holotype: United States National
Museum.
TYPE LOCALITY. Arkansas: Polk County; unidentified
springs on Rich Mountain, Rich Mountain Station.
Collector: L. Hubricht. 26 April 1936.
DISTRIBUTION. Known only from the type locality.

Class Isopoda—Freshwater Isopods and Pill Bugs

Terrestrial isopods, commonly known as pill bugs, sow
bugs, or roly-polys, are generally familiar to most of us.
Approximately 5 percent of North American isopod
species may be found in freshwater. The United States
is inhabited by about eighty freshwater species. Such
aquatic sow bugs or isopods range from 5 mm to 20
mm, are strongly flattened dorsoventrally, and the head
and first thoracic segment are fused. The seven remaining thoracic segments are similar and are expanded laterally. The last four abdominal segments are the true
telson and are completely fused. In Arkansas, only four
of the twenty-one known aquatic isopod species are
endemic to the state (Robison and Schram 1987). No
state endemic terrestrial isopod species are known.

Caecidotea fonticulus Lewis 1983: 149
Abernathy Spring Isopod
FIGURES 6.5, 6.6, 6.7

This isopod is the first troglobitic asellid to be found
from the Ouachita Mountains (Lewis 1983). It was discovered by Dr. Henry W. Robison during a survey of
the springs of the Ouachitas. *C. fonticulus* lives in
Abernathy Spring, a small spring which joins Big Fork
Creek a few meters from its source. Abernathy Spring
water temperature averages about 16°C and has a pH
of 7.0, conductivity of 144 ohms, and alkalinity of
70 mg/1 CaCo$_3$.

This zoogeographically interesting isopod can be
readily assigned to the *Hobbsi* group and is most closely

FIG. 6.5. Distribution of *Caecidotea fonticulus.*

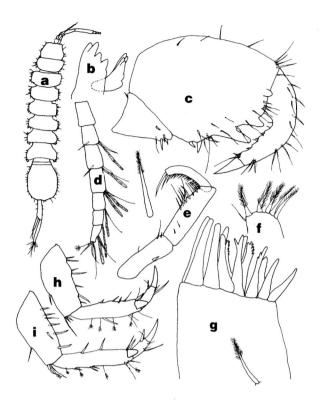

FIG. 6.6. *Caecidotea fonticulus*: a–h from male paratypes, i from female paratype. a, habitus, dorsal; b, incisor and lacinia, left mandible; c, pereiopod 1; d, antenna 1, distal segments; e, mandibular palp; f, maxilla 1, inner lobe; h, pereiopod 4, distal segments; i, same. *Redrawn from Lewis 1983.*

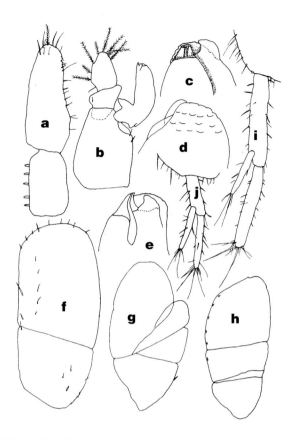

FIG. 6.7. *Caecidotea fonticulus*: a–i from male paratypes, j from female paratype. a, pleopod 1; b, pleopod 2; c–e, same, endopod tip, anterior, posterior, lateral views; f, pleopod 3; g, pleopod 4; h, pleopod 5; i, uropod; j, same. *Redrawn from Lewis 1983.*

related to *Caecidotea spatulata* and *C. fustis*, both Ozark species (Lewis 1983).

TYPE DEPOSITORY. Holotype: USNM 191128, United States National Museum. Date: 31 May 1981. J. J. Lewis and T. M. Lewis.

TYPE LOCALITY. Arkansas: Polk County; Abernathy Spring, N side of Hwy. 8, 0.8 mi. W of Polk-Montgomery County line.

DISTRIBUTION. Known only from the type locality.

Caecidotea holti Fleming 1972: 221

FIGURES 6.8, 6.9

Fleming (1972) described this rare isopod from specimens collected earlier in 1970 by Leslie Hubricht. *C. holti* has its closest affinities with *C. stiladactyla* and *C. dentadactyla*. This isopod inhabits small streams in Perry County in central Arkansas. Nothing is known about its biology.

TYPE DEPOSITORY. Holotype: USNM 790308, United States National Museum.

FIG. 6.8. Distribution of *Caecidotea holti*.

TYPE LOCALITY. Arkansas: Perry County; small stream 1.8 mi. E of Casa. Date: 4 May 1940. Collector: Leslie Hubricht.

DISTRIBUTION. Known only from the type locality.

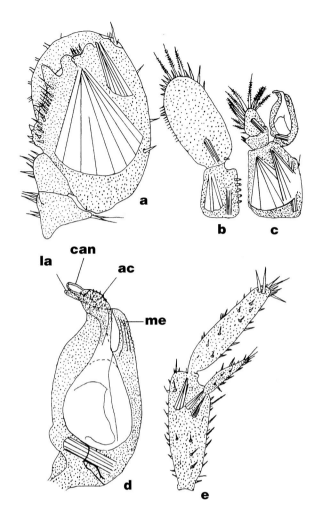

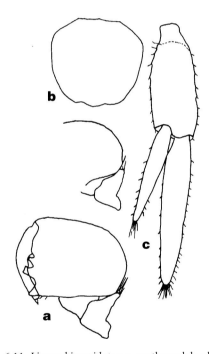

FIG. 6.10. Distribution of *Lirceus bicuspidatus*.

FIG. 6.9. *Caecidotea holti*: a, lateral view of distal podomeres of male left gnathopod; b, cephalic view of left pleopod 1; c, cephalic view of male left pleopod 2 ; d, cephalic view of tip of endopodite of male left pleopod 2; can—cannula; la—lateral process; me—mesial process; ac—accessory process; e, dorsal view of male left uropod. *Redrawn from Fleming 1972.*

Lirceus bicuspidatus Hubricht and Mackin 1949: 345

FIGURES 6.10, 6.11

This isopod inhabits a variety of aquatic biotopes from small seeps, springs, and streams to cave streams. Nothing more is known concerning the biology of this species, although it has a fairly wide distribution in the mountainous regions.

TYPE DEPOSITORY. Unknown.
TYPE LOCALITY. Arkansas: Johnson County; small stream flowing behind college chapel in Clarksville.
DISTRIBUTION. Arkansas: Conway, Jackson, Logan, Newton, Pope, Pulaski, Searcy, Yell.

FIG. 6.11. *Lirceus bicuspidatus*: a, gnathopod; b, pleotelson; c, uropod. *Redrawn from Hubricht and Mackin 1949.*

Lirceus bidentatus Hubricht and Mackin 1949: 344

FIGURES 6.12, 6.13

This is the only species which can be distinguished by the second pleopod of the male. In all species there is a depression in the tip of the endopodite, and in its center is a slender process. In most species this process barely projects above the rim of the depression. In *L. bidentatus* this process is greatly enlarged, equaling in length the diameter of the endopodite.

Because this species is known from only one seep in the Boston Mountains, virtually nothing is known about its biology.

TYPE DEPOSITORY. Unknown.
TYPE LOCALITY. Arkansas: Boone County; a seep in the Boston Mts., 9 mi. SW of Harrison. Collector: Leslie Hubricht.
DISTRIBUTION. Known only from the type locality.

FIG. 6.12. Distribution of *Lirceus bidentatus.*

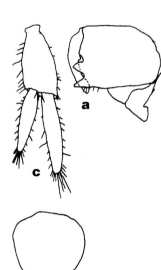

FIG. 6.13. *Lirceus bidentatus*: a, gnathopod; b, pleotelson; c, uropod. *Redrawn from Hubricht and Mackin 1949.*

Class Decapoda—Shrimps and Crayfishes

There are approximately fourteen species of shrimps and three hundred species and subspecies of crayfishes making up the Order Decapoda in the continental United States. These decapod crustaceans are common members of our aquatic communities in Arkansas. Although there are no endemic shrimps known from the state, fifteen endemic species of crayfishes do occur here. This is out of an incredible variety of fifty-six species and subspecies of crayfish within the state.

Crayfishes are easily recognized; therefore, a description is not presented here. However, it is important to point out that the taxonomy of North American crayfishes is based on numerous morphological characteristics, chief among which are the secondary sexual characteristics. The morphology of the male first pleopods is the single most important characteristic in identifying the species (Bouchard and Robison 1980). Adult males exist in two morphological forms: form I is capable of breeding, and form II is sexually nonfunctional. Form I males are important in determining if a new species is at hand, because taxonomic diagnostic characters are based solely on reproductive males.

Bouchardina robisoni Hobbs 1977: 734
FIGURES 6.14, 6.15

Bouchardina is the most recently discovered crayfish genus and is represented by a single species, *B. robisoni* (Hobbs 1977). This unique, small crayfish (about 3 cm) inhabits ditches, flooded grassy areas along the sides of roads, and small intermittent streams (0.66 m wide or less). Substrates include areas of sandy clay covered with decaying leaves. *Ludwigia* sp., *Utricularia* sp., and grasses are conspicuous aquatic plants. A tertiary burrower during periods of low water levels, *B. robisoni* has been collected from burrows of over 3 meters deep.

Form I males (reproductive males) have been collected in June and July. Ovigerous females (with eggs) have been taken in May. Little else is known of its biology.

This is a small species. The largest specimen known is a male with a carapace length of 16.6 mm (postorbital carpace length 11.4 mm.)

TYPE DEPOSITORY. Holotype: United States National Museum.
TYPE LOCALITY. Arkansas: Lafayette County; a borrow ditch along Sunray Road, 4 mi. N of Lewisville off Rte. 29 (Sec. 14, R24W, T15S). Date: 26 April 1975. Collectors: H. W. Robison, R. W. Bouchard, and H. H. Hobbs Jr.
DISTRIBUTION. Arkansas: Lafayette, Hempstead, Nevada, Columbia.

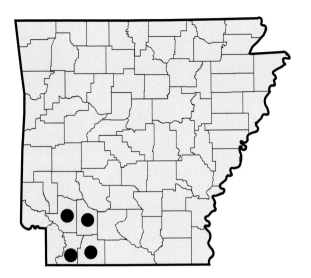

FIG. 6.14. Distribution of *Bouchardina robisoni*.

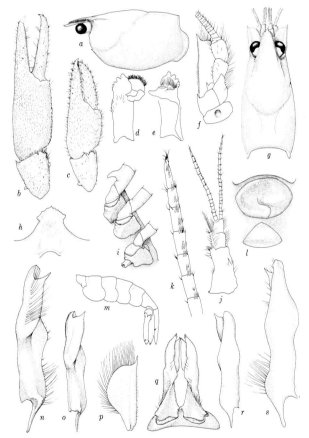

FIG. 6.15. *Bouchardina robisoni*: a, b, g, h, i, m, n, s from holotype; l from allotype; o, r from morphotype; c–f, j, k, p from paratypic female; q from paratypic male. a, lateral view of carapace; b, c, dorsal view of distal podomeres of cheliped; d, e, pre- and postaxial view of mandible, respectively; f, ventral view of proximal part of antenna; g, dorsal view of cephalothorax; h, epistome; e, basal podomeres of pereiopods 3, 4, 5; j, ventral view of antennule; k, ventral view of distal articles of lateral ramus of antennule; l, Annulus ventralis; m, lateral view of abdomen; n, o, mesial view of pleopod 1; p, antennal scale; q, caudal view of first pleopods; r, s, lateral view of pleopod 1. *From Hobbs 1977.*

Cambarus aculabrum Hobbs and Brown 1987: 1040

FIGURES 6.16, 6.17

This crayfish is only the second troglobitic decapod to be reported from Arkansas, the other is *Cambarus zophonastes* from Hell Creek Cave, Stone County (Hobbs and Brown 1987). *Cambarus aculabrum* is a member of the subgenus *Jugicambarus* and is one of only five species of the genus *Cambarus* inhabiting the state.

Cambarus aculabrum is known from only two localities: Logan Cave, the type locality, and Bear Hollow Cave, 38 km north northwest of Logan Cave. Logan Cave is an Ozarkian solution channel located in the Mississippian cherty-limestone Boone Formation of the Springfield Plateau. It is approximately 2000 m long, and water flows (19,000 m³/day) through the entire length as a brook at an elevation of about 323 m (Hobbs and Brown 1987). Most *C. aculabrum* have been seen in a pool formed by the collapse of the cave roof. They are generally found along the side walls of the pool or at the stream margin. Six was the largest number seen at one time.

The largest specimen available to date is a female with a carapace length of 28.2 mm (postorbital carapace length 24.0 mm). Form I males were collected on 31 December 1985, 16 January 1986, 20 February 1986, 8 October 1986, and 25 February 1987. Females carrying eggs or young have not been observed (Hobbs and Brown 1987).

TYPE DEPOSITORY. Holotype: USNM 219149, United States National Museum.

FIG. 6.16. Distribution of *Cambarus aculabrum*.

TYPE LOCALITY. Arkansas: Benton County; Logan Cave, about 11 km E of Siloam Springs (Gallatin Quadrangle T18N, R32W, Sec. 33). Collector: C. S. Todd.

DISTRIBUTION. Arkansas: Benton County; Logan Cave and Bear Hollow Cave.

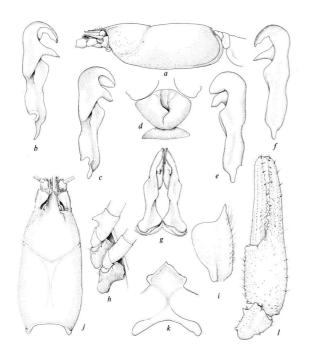

FIG. 6.17. *Cambarus aculabrum*: a, b, f–l from holotype; c, e from morphotype; and d from allotype. a, lateral view of cephalothorax; b, c, mesial view of pleopod 1; d, annulus ventralis; e, f, lateral view of pleopod 1; g, caudal view of first pleopods; h, ventral view of basal podomeres of pereiopods 3, 4; i, right antennal scale; j, dorsal view of carapace; k, epistome; l, dorsal view of distal podomeres of cheliped. *From Hobbs and Brown 1987.*

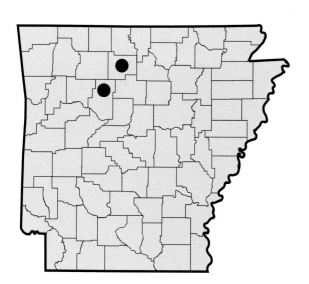

FIG. 6.18. Distribution of *Cambarus causeyi*.

Cambarus causeyi Reimer 1966: 9

FIGURES 6.18, 6.19, 6.20

This relict is a highly adapted crayfish that inhabits complex burrows on hillsides near springs in the Boston Mountains (Bouchard and Robison 1980). Dr. Henry W. Robison has taken specimens of this species from under boulders lying in a dry intermittent creek drainage and from under a rock in a spring filled with watercress. Burrows normally have several openings leading to a common tunnel that descends almost vertically (Reimer 1966). *Cambarus causeyi*, a member of the subgenus *Jugicambarus*, has its closest affinities to three troglobitic species: *Cambarus setosus*, *C. zophonastes* (Reimer 1966), and *C. aculabrum* (Hobbs and Brown 1987). However, *C. causeyi* is unique in having its body strongly compressed within the subgenus. Because few collections have been made of this species within Arkansas, *C. causeyi* remains one of the most little-known crayfishes.

TYPE DEPOSITORY. Holotype: USNM 116678, United States National Museum.

TYPE LOCALITY. Arkansas: Pope County; spring and natural pond, 4 mi. W of Sandgap on Hwy. 124. Collector: R. Reimer.

DISTRIBUTION. Arkansas: Pope, Searcy.

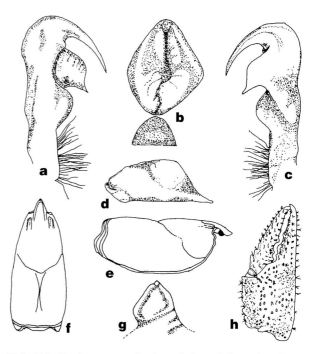

FIG. 6.19. *Cambarus causeyi*: a, lateral view of pleopod 1 of holotypic male; b, annulus ventralis; c, mesial view of pleopod 1 of holotypic male; d, antennal scale of holotypic male; e, lateral view of carapace of holotypic male; f, dorsal view of carapace of holotypic male; g, epistome of holotypic male; h, upper surface of chela of holotypic male. *Redrawn from Reimer 1966.*

FIG. 6.20. *Cambarus causeyi.* Photograph by Raymond W. Bouchard.

Cambarus zophonastes Hobbs and Bedinger 1964: 11

FIGURES 6.21, 6.22, 6.23

Cambarus zophonastes, a troglobitic crayfish, inhabits subterranean streams in Hell Creek Cave in Stone County. Hell Creek Cave is about 1500 feet long and was formed in plattin limestone during the Ordovician Age. The temperature of the water inside the cave has been measured at 56–58° F and flows at about 200 gallons per minute. An obligate cave dweller, *C. zophonastes* lacks pigment in the body, has long, thin appendages, reduced body size, and small eyes. The entire population is estimated to be fewer than 50 individuals.

Because the recharge area of the cave is quite large and groundwater contamination is a major potential threat to the crayfish, this species was proposed for

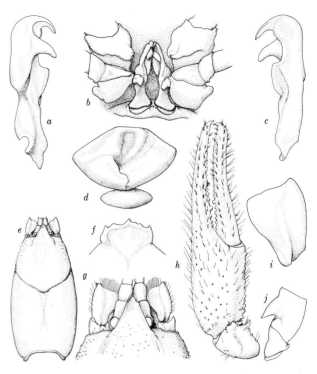

FIG. 6.22. *Cambarus zophonastes:* a, mesial view of first pleopod of male, form I; b, bases of fourth and fifth pereiopods and first pleopods of male, form I; c, lateral view of first pleopod of male, form I; d, annulus ventralis; e, dorsal view of carapace; f, epistome; g, dorsal view of cephalic region; h, distal podomeres of cheliped of male, form I; i, antennal scale; j, basipodite and ischiopodite of third pereiopod of male, form I. *From Hobbs and Bedinger 1964.*

FIG. 6.23. *Cambarus zophonastes.* Photograph by David Porter.

FIG. 6.21. Distribution of *Cambarus zophonastes.*

listing as endangered on 5 May 1986 and appeared on the list 7 April 1987. Fortunately, Hell Creek Cave was recently purchased by the Arkansas Natural Heritage Commission and the Nature Conservancy.

TYPE DEPOSITORY. Holotype: USNM 108356, United States National Museum.

TYPE LOCALITY. Arkansas: Stone County; Hell Creek Cave.

DISTRIBUTION. Arkansas: Known only from the type locality.

Fallicambarus harpi Hobbs and Robison 1985: 1035

FIGURES 6.24, 6.25

The crayfish *Fallicambarus harpi* was described by Hobbs and Robison (1985) from specimens collected in Pike County, Arkansas. It is a member of the subgenus *Fallicambarus* and is specifically distinguished by a combination of three characteristics: the cephalic process of the first pleopod extends caudodistally, hooks are only in the ischia of the third pereiopods, and the distomedian spine in the mesial ramus of the uropod is absent.

All specimens were collected in the early evening as they crawled about in wet grassy areas (Hobbs and Robison 1985). The sedges and grasses of the type locality are predominant with *Pinus*, *Quercus*, and *Cornus florida*. The burrows are simple in sandy clay soil.

The largest specimen known to date is a female that measured 39.6 mm in carapace length and 35.8 mm in postorbital length. The smallest and largest form I males have a carapace length of 29.0 mm and

35.4 mm and postorbital lengths of 25.8 mm and 31.5 mm, respectively.

TYPE DEPOSITORY. Holotype: USNM 217946, United States National Museum.

TYPE LOCALITY. Arkansas: Pike County; seepage area located 0.2 mi. E of Glenwood (Sec. 1, R24W, T5S) on Hwy. 70. Date: 21 April 1982. Collector: K. Dillard.

DISTRIBUTION. Arkansas: Pike, two localities.

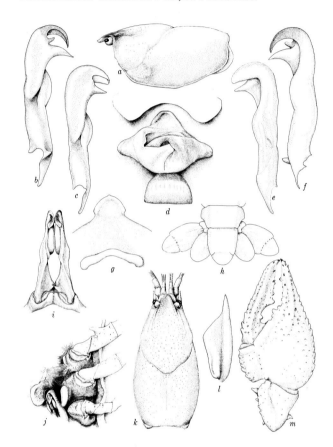

FIG. 6.25. *Fallicambarus harpi*: a, b, f, i, g, h, j, k, l, m from holotype; c, e from morphotype; d from allotype. a, lateral view of carapace; b, c, mesial view of pleopod 1; d, annulus ventralis and adjacent sternal features; e, f, lateral view of pleopod 1; g, epistome; h, dorsal view of telson and uropods; i, caudal view of first pleopods; j, ventrolateral view of basal podomeres of pereiopods 3, 4, 5 and first pleopods; k, dorsal view of carapace; l, right antennal scale; m, dorsal view of distal podomeres of pereiopod 1. *From Hobbs 1975.*

FIG. 6.24. Distribution of *Fallicambarus harpi*.

Fallicambarus caesius Hobbs 1975: 24

FIGURES 6.26, 6.27

This bluish gray burrowing member of the subgenus *Creaserinus* was originally described by Hobbs (1975) and is widely distributed in southern Arkansas. Form I males have been collected in February, April, May, and November (Hobbs and Robison 1989). Ovigerous (egg carrying) females have been found in February and

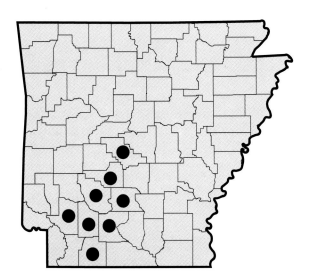

FIG. 6.26. Distribution of *Fallicambarus caesius.*

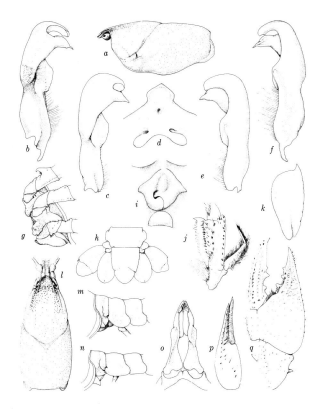

FIG. 6.27. *Fallicambarus caesius:* c, e from morphotype; i, n from allotype; all others from holotype. a, lateral view of carapace; b, mesial view of pleopod 1; c, same; d, epistome; e, lateral view of pleopod 1; f, same ; g, basal podomeres of pereiopods 3, 4, 5; h, dorsal view of caudal part of abdomen; i, annulus ventralis; j, ventral view of basis and ischium of maxilliped 3; k, antennal scale; l, dorsal view of carapace; m, lateral view of cephalic segments of abdomen; n, same; o, caudal view of first pleopods; p, ventrolateral view of propodus of chela showing row of setal tufts; q, dorsal view of distal podomeres of cheliped. *From Hobbs 1975.*

April. *F. caesius* inhabits highly branched burrows in rain-soaked soil consisting generally of clay, organic material, and occasionally gravel. Sedges and grasses usually occur in the immediate vicinity of the burrow.

F. caesius has its closest affinities with *F. gilpini.* The two species are the only typically blue members of the genus *Fallicambarus* and lack a ventrolateral row of tubercles on the merus of the first cheliped. It can be distinguished from *F. gilpini* by the absence of tubercles on the mesial surface of the dactyl of the chela and the presence of a distolateral spine on the mesial ramus of the uropod.

TYPE LOCALITY. Arkansas: Saline County; roadside ditch at the Hot Spring County line on Hwy. 67. Date: 22 April 1973. Collectors: H. H. Hobbs and J. E. Pugh. TYPE DEPOSITORY. Holotype: USNM 144921, United States National Museum.
DISTRIBUTION. Arkansas: Clark, Columbia, Dallas, Hempstead, Hot Spring, Nevada, Ouachita, Saline.

Fallicambarus jeanae Hobbs 1973: 463
FIGURES 6.28, 6.29, 6.30

Fallicambarus jeanae exhibits two color morphs. The first is described as follows: the dominant color of the carapace is pale mauve and the caudal margin of the carapace is dark brown; the first abdominal tergum is dark brown and the remaining ones are a pale yellowish tan; the telson and uropods are cream colored with a pale tan suffusion basally; and the cheliped is mostly yellowish tan dorsally with dark bluish brown tubercules.(Hobbs and Robison 1989).

The second color morph was originally described by Hobbs (1973) as a separate species, *Fallicambarus spectrum*, previously considered a state endemic (Robison and Smith 1982). The second color morph is described as follows: the dominant color of the carapace is a pale mauve gray with the caudal margin edged with black; the first abdominal tergum is a reddish brown with the others fading to uniformly reddish tan telson and uropods; and the chelipeds are grayish blue dorsally with dark blue tubercules. Hobbs and Robison (1989) recently concluded that this form should be treated as a color morph of *F. jeanae.*

The largest specimen available is a female with a carapace length of 40.6 mm with a postorbital length of 35.5 mm. Smallest and largest form I males have corresponding lengths of 30 (26.4) mm and 35.7 (31.7) mm, respectively (Hobbs and Robison 1989).

This species inhabits complex burrows with two or three openings to the surface. The burrows are in sandy

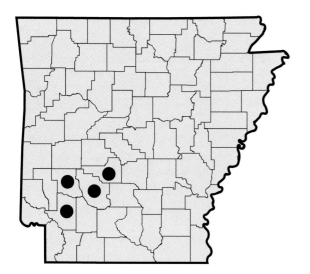

FIG. 6.28. Distribution of *Fallicambarus jeanae.*

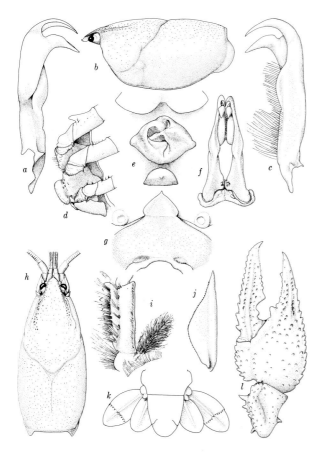

FIG. 6.29. *Fallicambarus jeanae:* new species (pubescence removed from all structures illustrated except c, d, i; all depict holotype except e, f, i). a, mesial view of pleopod 1; b, lateral view of carapace; c, lateral view of pleopod 1; d, basal podomeres of pereiopods 3, 4, 5; e, annulus ventralis of allotype; f, caudal view of first pleopods of paratypic form I male; g, epistome; h, dorsal view of carapace; i, basal podomeres of maxilliped 3 of paratypic form I male; j, antennal scale; k, dorsal view of telson and uropods; l, dorsal view of distal podomeres of cheliped. *From Hobbs 1973.*

clay with shallow pockets rich in organic material and some gravel. Grasses, sedges, and stands of *Acer, Junipers,* and *Pinus* generally surround the burrows.

TYPE DEPOSITORY. Holotype: USNM 144674, United States National Museum.

TYPE LOCALITY. Arkansas: Clark County; seepage area 1.8 mi. E of Clark County line on Rte. 84, Hot Spring County. Collectors: H. H. Hobbs Jr., G. Hobbs, and J. E. Pugh.

DISTRIBUTION. Arkansas: Clark, Hot Spring, Hempstead, Pike.

FIG. 6.30. *Fallicambarus jeanae. Photograph by Raymond W. Bouchard.*

Fallicambarus gilpini Hobbs and Robison 1989: 684

FIGURES 6.31, 6.32

Fallicambarus gilpini was recently described by Hobbs and Robison (1989) in Jefferson County, Arkansas. This species has been collected from complex burrows consisting of branching galleries, several of which reach the surface. Hobbs and Robison (1989) speculate that *F. gilpini* might prefer areas in which the groundwater is moving, as opposed to areas in which the water is more static.

Biologically, little is known concerning *F. gilpini.* Three ovigerous females were collected on 11 March 1988. Eggs were about 2 mm in diameter. No form I males have been collected in the field.

F. gilpini has its closest relationships with *F. caesius.* They are the only typically blue members of the genus and both lack a ventrolateral row of tubercules on the merus of the first cheliped.

TYPE DEPOSITORY. Holotype: USNM 219511, United States National Museum.

TYPE LOCALITY. Arkansas: Jefferson County; roadside seepage, 3.1 mi. S of Rte. 54 on Hwy. 79, approximately

11 mi. S of Pine Bluff. Collector: H. W. Robison. Date: 18 March 1987.

DISTRIBUTION. Known only from the type locality.

FIG. 6.31. Distribution of *Fallicambarus gilpini.*

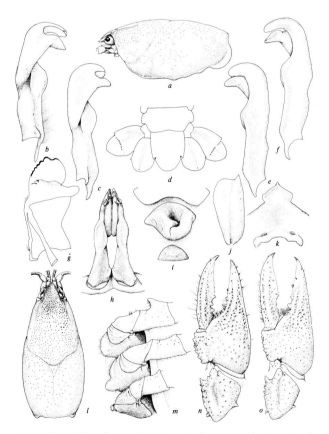

FIG. 6.32. *Fallicambarus gilpini*: c and e from morphotype; i and n from allotype; all others from holotype. a, lateral view of cara-pace; b, c, mesial view of pleopod 1; d, dorsal view of caudal part of abdomen; e, f, lateral view of pleopod 1; g, postaxial view of mandible; h, caudal view of first pleopods; i, annulus ventralis and associated sclerites; j, antennal scale; k, epistome; l, dorsal view of carapace; n, basal podomeres of pereiopods 3, 4, 5; n, o, distal podomeres of cheliped. *From Hobbs and Robison 1989.*

Fallicambarus petilicarpus Hobbs and Robison 1989: 661

FIGURES 6.33, 6.34, 6.35

Fallicambarus petilicarpus was recently described by Hobbs and Robison (1989) in one locality in Union County, Arkansas. This beautiful burrowing crayfish has a dark olive brown carapace and first abdominal tergum with the second through fifth abdominal tergum paler olive tan. Tergum and uropods are dark olive. Chelipeds are pinkish cream with green dorsal tubercles with white tips.

The largest specimen known is a female with a carapace length of 31.8 mm and a postorbital length of 27.6 mm. The smallest form I male has a 30.5 mm carapace length and a 26.6 mm postorbital length. No females are available that are ovigerous or are carrying young.

Fallicambarus petilicarpus is more closely allied to *F. dissitus* than to any other member of the genus (Hobbs and Robison 1989).

TYPE DEPOSITORY. Holotype: USNM 219507, United States National Museum.

TYPE LOCALITY. Arkansas: Union County; roadside seepage 0.2 mi. E of the Columbia County line on Rte. 57. Collector: H. W. Robison. Date: 28 March 1988.

DISTRIBUTION. Known only from the type locality.

FIG. 6.33. Distribution of *Fallicambarus petilicarpus.*

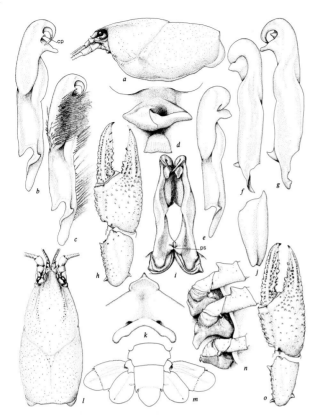

FIG. 6.34. *Fallicambarus petilicarpus*: d, h, j from allotype; e, f from morphotype; all others from holotype. a, lateral view of carapace; b, c, e, mesial view of pleopod 1; cp, cephalic process; d, annulus ventralis and associated sclerites; f, g, lateral view of pleopod 1; h, o, distal podomeres of cheliped; i, caudal view of first pleopods; j, antennal scale; k, epistome; l, dorsal view of carapace; m, dorsal view of caudal part of abdomen; n, basal podomeres of pereiopods 3, 4, 5; (cp, cephalic process; ps, proximomesial spur). *From Hobbs and Robison 1989.*

FIG. 6.35. *Fallicambarus petilicarpus.* Photograph by Henry W. Robison.

Fallicambarus strawni (Reimer) 1966: 11

FIGURES 6.36, 6.37, 6.38

This pinkish cream to purplish tan crayfish was originally described in the genus *Cambarus* by Reimer (1966). Hobbs (1969) later used *C. strawni* as the type species for his proposed taxon of *Fallicambarus*. He assigned an assemblage of eight species to *Fallicambarus* that were formerly assigned to the genus *Cambarus*. *F. strawni* is a member of the subgenus *Fallicambarus*.

The largest specimen available is a female with a carapace length of 37.2 mm and a postorbital length of 32.4 mm (Hobbs and Robison 1989). The largest form I male has a carapace length of 31.9 mm. Form I males have been collected in April and June. Ovigerous females have not been observed.

Burrows are highly branched (complex) in marshy areas with sandy clay soil. Colonies are generally small (4–9 burrows). Individuals have also been found in seepage areas.

TYPE DEPOSITORY. Holotype: USNM 116675, United States National Museum.
TYPE LOCALITY. Arkansas: Howard County; small marshy area in the Saline River drainage 2.7 mi. N of Dierks. Date: 22 June 1963. Collector: R. D. Reimer.
DISTRIBUTION. Arkansas: Howard, Pike.

FIG. 6.36. Distribution of *Fallicambarus strawni.*

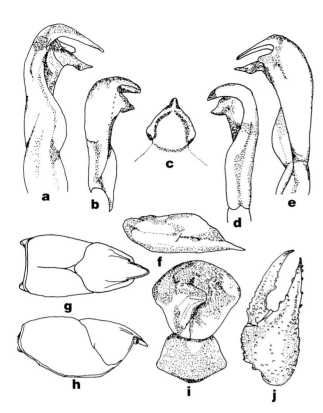

FIG. 6.37. *Fallicambarus strawni*: a, lateral view of pleopod 1 of holotypic male; b, mesial view of pleopod 1 of morphotypic male; c, epistome of holotypic male; d, lateral view of pleopod 1 of morphotypic male; e, mesial view of pleopod 1 of holotypic male; f, antennal scale of holotypic male; g, dorsal view of carapace of holotypic male; h, lateral view of carapace of holotypic male; i, annulus ventralis; j, upper surface of chela of holotypic male. *Redrawn from Reimer 1966.*

FIG. 6.38. *Fallicambarus strawni. Photograph by Raymond W. Bouchard.*

Orconectes acares Fitzpatrick 1965: 87

FIGURES 6.39, 6.40, 6.41

This small crayfish is common in the clear tributaries of the upper Ouachita River system draining from the Ouachita Mountains. This form was originally described as a subspecies, *Orconectes leptogonopodus acares* by Fitzpatrick (1965), although no evidence of integrade populations was found at the time. *Orconectes acares* may be distinguished from *O. leptogonopodus* by a shorter pleopod and a shorter and smaller central projection. The mesial process ratio mean value for *acares* is 1:34; for *leptogonopodus*: it is 1:43.

O. *acares* generally inhabits the runs or riffle areas of streams. Little else is known of its biology.

TYPE DEPOSITORY. Holotype: USNM 115517, United States National Museum.
TYPE LOCALITY. Arkansas: Montgomery County; stream tributary to Ouachita River 6 mi. NW of Mt. Ida.
DISTRIBUTION. Arkansas: Garland, Hot Spring, Montgomery, Perry, Pike, Polk, Saline.

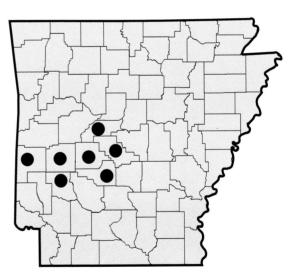

FIG. 6.39. Distribution of *Orconectes acares.*

Procambarus ferrugineus Hobbs and Robison 1988: 391

FIGURES 6.42, 6.43

This beautiful crayfish was originally described by Hobbs and Robison (1988) from specimens collected in Lonoke County. It is a member of the *gracilis* group of the subgenus *Girardiella.*

Specimens have been collected from simple or bifid galleries topped by crude chimneys as tall as

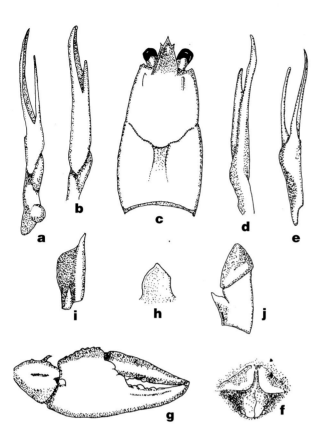

FIG. 6.42. Distribution of *Procambarus ferrugineus*.

FIG. 6.40. *Orconectes acares*: a, mesial view of pleopod 1 of holotype; b, mesial view of pleopod 1 of morphotype; c, dorsal view of carapace of holotype; d, lateral view of pleopod 1 of morphotype; e, lateral view of pleopod 1 of holotype; f, annulus ventralis of allotype; g, upper view of right chela of holotype; h, epistome of holotype; i, antennal scale of holotype; j, basipodite and ischiopodite of pereiopod 3 showing hook. (Mesial process of holotype slightly warped in preservation; in life, it is less divergent and is straight.) *Redrawn from Fitzpatrick 1965.*

FIG. 6.41. *Orconectes acares*. Photograph by Raymond W. Bouchard.

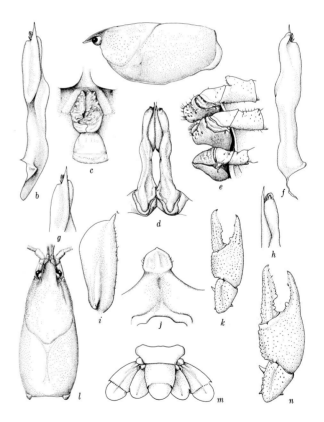

FIG. 6.43. *Procambarus ferrugineus*: c, k from allotype; b, f–h from paratypic form I male; all others from holotype. a, lateral view of carapace; b, submesial view of pleopod 1; c, annulus ventralis and associated sclerites; d, caudal view of first pleopods; e, ventral view of basal podomeres of pereiopods 3, 4, 5; f, sublateral view of pleopod 1; g, submesial view of distal part of pleopod 1; h, caudal view of distal part of pleopod; i, dorsal view of antennal scale; j, epistome; k, dorsal view of distal podomeres of cheliped; l, dorsal view of carapace; m, dorsal view of telson and uropods; n, dorsal view of distal podomeres of cheliped. *From Hobbs and Robison 1988.*

15 cm. The burrows penetrated the water table 20–25 cm below the surface and descended to depths of 1 m (Hobbs and Robison 1988). Soils were sandy clay over clay. Nothing else is known about the biology of this species.

TYPE DEPOSITORY. Holotype: USNM 218841, United States National Museum.
TYPE LOCALITY. Arkansas: Lonoke County; roadside ditch 10 mi. (16 km) S of Lonoke on Hwy. 31 (T1S, R8W, Sec. 6). Date: 16 April 1985. Collector: H. H. Hobbs Jr.
DISTRIBUTION. Arkansas: Lonoke, two localities.

Procambarus liberorum Fitzpatrick 1978: 533

FIGURES 6.44, 6.45

This crayfish is a member of the subgenus *Girardiella* which burrows in the soft sediments of the Boston Mountains and Arkansas River valley. Originally described by Fitzpatrick (1978) from only three specimens caught by a cat in a Bentonville yard, Hobbs and Robison (1988) recently extended the range of this primary burrower to cover eight counties in northwest Arkansas.

Form I males have been collected in April and May; however, little else is known of the biology of this species.

TYPE DEPOSITORY. Holotype: USNM 148353, United States National Museum.
TYPE LOCALITY. Arkansas: Benton County, Bentonville.
DISTRIBUTION. Arkansas: Benton, Washington, Franklin, Logan, Pope, Scott, Sebastian, Yell.

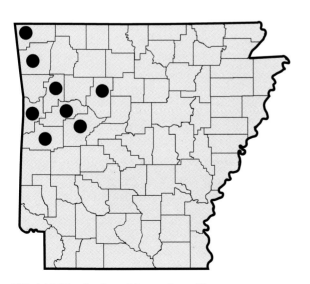

FIG. 6.44. Distribution of *Procambarus liberorum*.

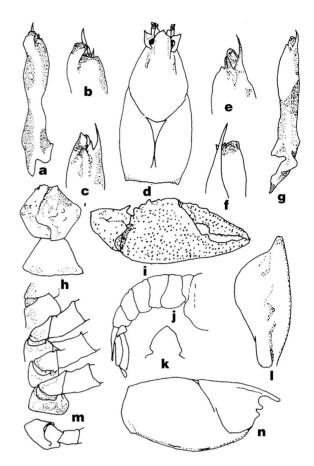

FIG. 6.45. *Procambarus liberorum:* a, lateral view of first pleopod; b, lateral view of terminal elements of first pleopod; c, cephalic view of terminal elements of first pleopod; d, dorsal view of carapace; e, mesial view of terminal elements of first pleopod; f, caudal view of terminal elements of first pleopod; g, mesial view of first pleopod; h, annulus ventralis and fifth sternite of allotype; i, upper view of distal podomeres of cheliped; j, lateral view of abdomen; k, cephalic part of epistome; l, upper view of antennal scale; m, proximal podomeres of left pereiopods; n, lateral view of carapace. *Redrawn from Fitzpatrick 1978.*

Procambarus regalis Hobbs and Robison 1988: 398

FIGURES 6.46, 6.47

Hobbs and Robison (1988) recently described this splendid species as having a brownish red carapace that contrasted strikingly with the orange to cream-orange lateral rostral ridges and postorbital ridges and a broad brownish red, laterally undulating stripe terminating on the telson.

The largest specimen collected to date is a form I male having a carapace length of 40.8 mm with a postorbital length of 36.3 mm.

This crayfish inhabits simple burrows constructed in a generally sandy clay soil which may extend to a

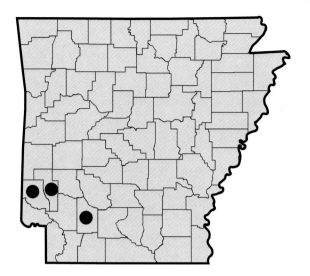

FIG. 6.46. Distribution of *Procambarus regalis*.

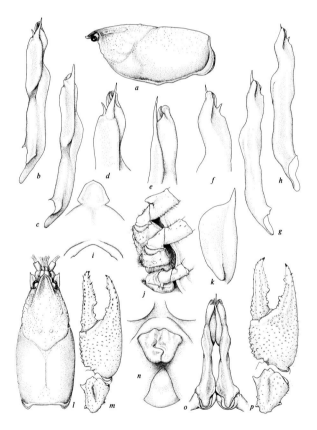

FIG. 6.47. *Procambarus regalis*: n, p from allotype; c, g from morphotype; all others from holotype. a, lateral view of carapace; b–d, mesial view of pleopod 1; e, caudal view of distal part of pleopod 1; f–h, lateral view of pleopod 1; i, epistome; j, ventral view of basal podomeres of pereiopods 3, 4, 5; k, dorsal view of antennal scale; l, dorsal view of carapace; m, p, dorsal view of distal podomeres of cheliped; n, annulus ventralis and assocaited sclerites; o, caudal view of first pleopods. *From Hobbs and Robison 1988.*

depth of 1 m and are topped by chimneys 8–12 cm high. Colonies may be extremely large, sometimes extending over whole unplowed fields of farms in southwestern Arkansas.

TYPE DEPOSITORY. Holotype: USNM 219244, United States National Museum.

TYPE LOCALITY. Arkansas: Nevada County; De Ann Cemetery, about 1 mi. (1.6 km) W of the junction of Hwys. 19 and 24 at the western city limit of Prescott (T11S, R22W, Sec. 8). Date: 16 March 1982. Collector: Elaine Laird.

DISTRIBUTION. Arkansas: Sevier, Howard, Nevada

Procambarus reimeri Hobbs 1979: 804

FIGURES 6.48, 6.49

Hobbs (1979) discovered this crayfish species in 1973 in Polk County; however, he did not officially describe it until six years later. *Procambarus reimeri*, a pinkish-cream colored burrowing crayfish, is a member of the subgenus *Girardiella* and is confined to the Ouachita River basin of Polk County (Hobbs and Robison 1988). Only six localities for this species in Polk County are known.

This crayfish inhabits relatively simple burrows, 0.50–1 m in depth, constructed in a sandy clay soil. Burrows are common in roadside ditches.

Procambarus reimeri has its closest affinities with *P. gracilis* and *P. liberorum*.

TYPE DEPOSITORY. Holotype: USNM 148880, United States National Museum.

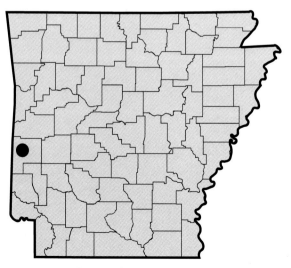

FIG. 6.48. Distribution of *Procambarus reimeri*.

TYPE LOCALITY. Arkansas: Polk County; burrows in a roadside ditch about 5 mi. NE of Mena on unnumbered road to Irons Fork River. Date: 18 April 1973. Collectors: H. H. Hobbs Jr., G. B. Hobbs, and J. E. Pugh.

DISTRIBUTION. Arkansas: Polk.

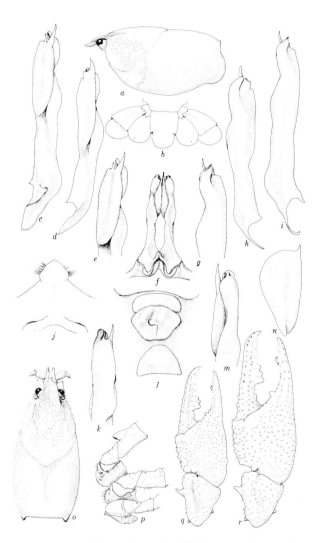

FIG. 6.49. *Procambarus reimeri*: d and h from morphotype; l and q from allotype; all others from holotype. a, lateral view of carapace; b, dorsal view of telson and uropods; c, d, e, mesial view of pleopod 1; f, caudal view of first pleopods; g, h, i, lateral view of pleopod 1; j, epistome; k, cephalic view of distal part of pleopod 1; l, annulus ventralis; m, caudal view of distal part of pleopod 1; n, antennal scale; o, dorsal view of carapace; p, basal podomeres of pereiopods 3, 4, 5; q, r, dorsal view of distal podomeres of cheliped. *From Hobbs 1979.*

7

Myriapoda
Millipedes and Relatives

Millipedes are one of the more obvious groups of ground-dwelling arthropods throughout Arkansas. They may be found in leaf litter, under rocks and bark, and in a variety of habitats ranging from very wet and moist to dry.

Except for a few species described by early workers in the 1800s, most of the Arkansas species have been described by N. B. Causey and R. V. Chamberlin. We would like to note that Nell B. Causey was the wife of David Causey. David Causey was a faculty member for many years in the Department of Zoology at the University of Arkansas, Fayetteville. Nell Causey never held a position with the university, probably because of archaic nepotism laws. Mrs. Causey deposited her type material in institutions outside of Arkansas and, upon her death, bequeathed her specimens and reprint collection to Florida State University.

There remains a great deal of work to be done with the millipede fauna of Arkansas and the Interior Highlands. Distribution records are far from complete. There are, no doubt, many taxa left to be discovered and described. We know virtually nothing about any of the cladistic and biogeographic relationships of the species or higher taxa in the class *Diplopoda*. Such cladistic/biogeographic studies would be highly informative and relevant to our understanding of the origin and history of the biota of North America.

Class Symphyla—Symphylans

Family Scutigerellidae

Hanseniella ouachiticha Allen 1992: 170
FIGURES 7.1, 7.2

The Symphyla are very small (1 to 5 mm), white organisms that live in the soil, under rocks and bark, and occasionally in leaf debris. Many of the species feed on the roots of various plants, while others appear to be scavengers that feed on a variety of organic matter. The genus *Hanseniella* contains about fifty species worldwide. In the United States there are only two additional species, both known only from California. *Hanseniella ouachiticha* can be distinguished from the other species by the smaller number of antennal segments, the short central rod in the head, and the three prominent setae on the proximal segment of the first pair of legs.

TYPE DEPOSITORY. Holotype: American Museum of Natural History. Paratypes: University of Arkansas Insect Collection.

TYPE LOCALITY. Arkansas: Polk; Rich Mountain, Eagleton Overlook.

DISTRIBUTION. Known only from the type locality.

FIG. 7.1. Distribution of *Hanseniella ouachiticha* in Arkansas.

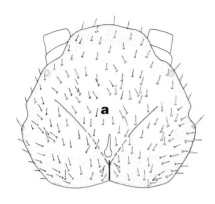
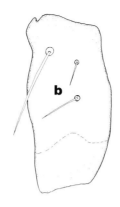

FIG. 7.2. *Hanseniella ouachiticha:* a, head, dorsal; b, proximal segment of first pair of legs (Allen 1992).

Order Polydesmida

Family Desmonidae

Desmonus pudicus (Bollman) 1888: 3

FIGURES 7.3, 7.4

This species was originally described and placed in the genus *Sphaeriodesus.* There is one additional species, *D. earlei,* in this genus in Alabama, Tennessee, and Kentucky, and one additional monotypic genus, *Desmoniella,* has been assigned to the *Desmonidae* family. *D. curta* Loomis was described from specimens collected in the Arbuckle Mountains in Pontotoc County, Oklahoma.

TYPE DEPOSITORY. USNM 154, United States National Museum.
TYPE LOCALITY. Arkansas: Pulaski County; Little Rock.
DISTRIBUTION. Arkansas: Clark, Pulaski.

FIG. 7.3. Distribution of *Desmonus pudicus.*

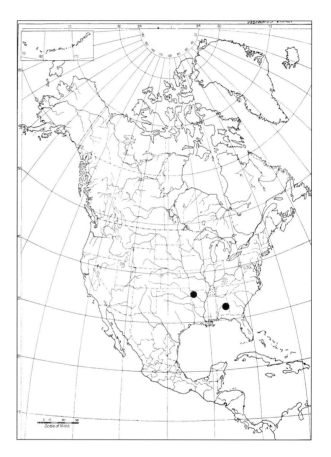

FIG. 7.4. Distribution of the genus *Desmonus* in North America.

Family Eurydesmidae

Cibularia profuga Causey 1955: 29

FIGURES 7.5, 7.6, 7.7

The type specimens—three males, three females, and one larva—were collected under rocks. This species was collected from an area of pine and hardwoods. There is one additional species in the genus, *C. tuobita* (Chamberlin), from Otero and Lincoln Counties in central New Mexico.

TYPE DEPOSITORY. American Museum of Natural History.
TYPE LOCALITY. Arkansas: Montgomery County; Mt. Ida, 5 mi. S of Ouachita River bridge. Date: 14 April 1954.
DISTRIBUTION. Known only from the type locality.

FIG. 7.5. Distribution of *Cibularia profuga*.

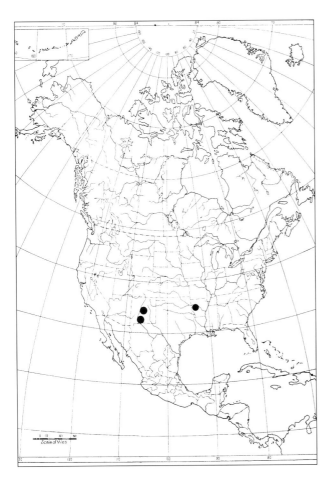

FIG. 7.6. Distribution of the genus *Cibularia* in North America.

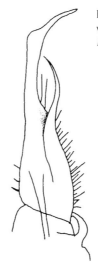

FIG. 7.7. *Cibularia profuga*: Subdorsal view of telopodite of left gonopod. *Redrawn from Causey 1955.*

Mimuloria davidcauseyi (Causey) 1950: 194

FIGURES 7.8, 7.9, 7.10

This species was originally placed in the genus *Nannaria.* Causey states that the "two recently molted males and two larvae were collected by Dr. David Causey on 25 August 1950 from an oak-hickory woodland on an east hillside." There are five species in this genus, three from the Ozark Mountains and one each from Ohio and Indiana.

TYPE DEPOSITORY. Philadelphia Academy of Sciences.
TYPE LOCALITY. Arkansas: Newton County; about 3 mi. NW of Jasper.
DISTRIBUTION. Known only from the type locality.

FIG. 7.8. Distribution of *Mimuloria davidcauseyi*.

FIG. 7.11. Distribution of *Mimuloria depalmai*.

Pleuroloma mirbila (Causey) 1951: 85

FIGURES 7.12, 7.13, 7.14

Causey noted that the habitat of this species was "rather dry litter on a north oak-hickory covered hillside." This species was originally placed in the genus *Zinaria*. Chamberlin and Hoffman (1958) note that there are twelve species in the genus, "most of which will probably be shown to be only geographic races of *P. flavipes*." All of the species in the genus are eastern in distribution.

TYPE DEPOSITORY. Philadelphia Academy of Sciences.
TYPE LOCALITY. Arkansas: Clay County; 12 mi. NE of Piggott on Hwy. 62.
DISTRIBUTION. Known only from the type locality.

FIG. 7.9. Distribution of the genus *Mimuloria* in North America.

FIG. 7.10. *Mimuloria davidcauseyi*: Telopodite of gonopod on male. *Redrawn from Causey 1950.*

Mimuloria depalmai (Causey) 1950: 1

FIGURE 7.11

The type locality, Lake Leatherwood, is east of Eureka Springs on Highway 62. The area has long been frequented by tourists and fishermen but has not been extensively developed. Wooded hillsides surround the lake and the nearby area. This species was originally described in the genus *Castanaria*.

TYPE DEPOSITORY. Philadelphia Academy of Sciences.
TYPE LOCALITY. Arkansas: Carroll County; 2 mi. S of Lake Leatherwood.
DISTRIBUTION. Known only from the type locality.

FIG. 7.12. Distribution of *Pleuroloma mirbila*.

FIG. 7.13. Distribution of the genus *Pleuroloma* in North America.

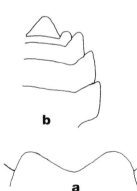

FIG. 7.14. *Pleuroloma mirbila*: a, sternal process between second pair of legs of thirteenth segment; b, tergites of last five segments. *Redrawn from Causey 1951.*

Family Euryuridae

The family Euryuridae is divided into two subfamilies. Members of the Aphelidesminae are predominately neotropical with one species known from Kerr County, Texas. Members of the Euryurinae are found only in eastern North America.

Auturus florus Causey 1950: 37

FIGURES 7.15, 7.16

There are ten species in this eastern genus. One species, *A. mimetes* Chamberlin, is endemic to Christian and

FIG. 7.15. Distribution of *Auturus florus.*

Jefferson Counties in Missouri. The type locality for *Auturus florus* is now within the Buffalo National River area and is thus protected. A special collecting permit is required.

TYPE DEPOSITORY. Philadelphia Academy of Sciences.
TYPE LOCALITY. Arkansas: Newton County; Compton, Hemmed-In Hollow.
DISTRIBUTION. Known only from the type locality.

FIG. 7.16. Distribution of the genus *Auturus* in North America.

Family Eurymerodesmidae

Eurymerodesmus angularis Causey 1951: 69

FIGURES 7.17, 7.18

There are twenty-one species in this genus. All of the species are found in eastern North America.

TYPE DEPOSITORY. Philadelphia Academy of Science.
TYPE LOCALITY. Arkansas: Prairie County.
DISTRIBUTION. Known only from the type locality.

FIG. 7.17. Distribution of *Eurymerodesmus angularis*.

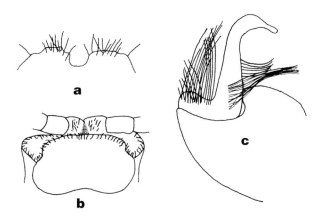

FIG. 7.18. *Eurymerodesmus angularis*: a, caudal view of sternum between ninth legs of male; b, ventral view of gonopodal opening; c, submedial view of left gonopod of male. *Redrawn from Causey 1951.*

Eurymerodesmus bentonus Causey 1950: 268

FIGURES 7.19, 7.20

Much of the area around the type locality, the Monte Ne community, has been flooded by the impoundment of Beaver Lake Reservoir. However, this species may still exist in habitats on the hillsides surrounding the Monte Ne area.

TYPE DEPOSITORY. Philadelphia Academy of Sciences.
TYPE LOCALITY. Arkansas: Benton County; Monte Ne.
DISTRIBUTION. Known only from the type locality.

FIG. 7.19. Distribution of *Eurymerodesmus bentonus*.

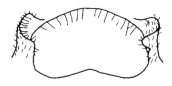

FIG. 7.20. *Eurymerodesmus bentonus*: Gonopodal opening (gonopods omitted), anterio-ventral view. *Redrawn from Causey 1950.*

Eurymerodesmus compressus Causey 1952: 38

FIGURES 7.21, 7.22

TYPE DEPOSITORY. Philadelphia Academy of Sciences.
TYPE LOCALITY. Arkansas: Union County; Junction City.
DISTRIBUTION. Known only from the type locality.

FIG. 7.21. Distribution of *Eurymerodesmus compressus*.

Eurymerodesmus dubius Chamberlin 1943: 38

FIGURES 7.23, 7.24

TYPE DEPOSITORY. Field Museum of Natural History, Chicago.
TYPE LOCALITY. Arkansas: Pike County; Delight. Date: 16 April 1941. Collector: K. P. Schmidt.
DISTRIBUTION. Arkansas: Clark, Dallas, Hot Spring, Pike, Saline, Sevier.

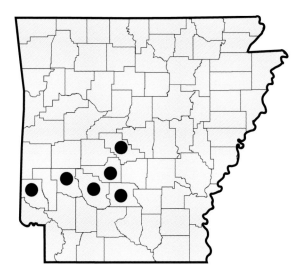

FIG. 7.23. Distribution of *Eurymerodesmus dubius*.

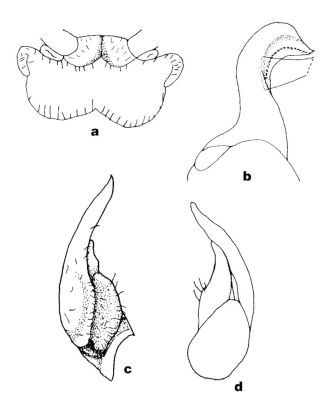

FIG. 7. 24. *Eurymerodesmus dubius*: Gonopod of male. *Redrawn from Chamberlin 1943.*

FIG. 7.22. *Eurymerodesmus compressus*: a, ventral view of out-line of gonopodal opening; b, mesial view of telopodite of left gonopod (setae of lateral and dorsal rows omitted, mesial row indicated); c, cephalic view of left vulva; d, caudal view of left vulva. *Redrawn from Causey 1950.*

Eurymerodesmus goodi Causey 1952: 3

FIGURE 7.25

TYPE DEPOSITORY. R. V. Chamberlin Collection.
TYPE LOCALITY. Arkansas: Polk County; 16 mi. SE of Mena.
DISTRIBUTION. Known only from the type locality.

FIG. 7.25. Distribution of *Eurymerodesmus goodi*.

Eurymerodesmus newtonius Chamberlin 1942: 6

FIGURE 7.26

TYPE DEPOSITORY. R. V. Chamberlin Collection.
TYPE LOCALITY. Arkansas: Newton County; 12 mi. S of Jasper.
DISTRIBUTION. Known only from the type locality.

FIG. 7.26. Distribution of *Eurymerodesmus newtonius*.

Eurymerodesmus oliphantus Chamberlin 1942: 6

FIGURE 7.27

TYPE DEPOSITORY. R. V. Chamberlin Collection.

TYPE LOCALITY. Arkansas: Jackson County; 15 mi. S of Liphant.
DISTRIBUTION. Known only from the type locality.

FIG. 7.27. Distribution of *Eurymerodesmus oliphantus*.

Eurymerodesmus schmidti Chamberlin 1943: 38

FIGURES 7.28, 7.29

TYPE DEPOSITORY. Field Museum of Natural History, Chicago.
TYPE LOCALITY. Arkansas: Polk County; Rich Mountain, elev. 2400 ft. Date: 22 March 1958. Collector: K. P. Schmidt.
DISTRIBUTION. Known only from the type locality.

FIG. 7.28. Distribution of *Eurymerodesmus schmidti*.

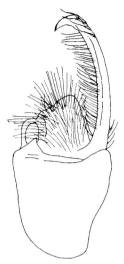

FIG. 7.29. *Eurymerodesmus schmidti*: Subanterior view of the male gonopod. *Redrawn from Chamberlin 1943.*

Eurymerodesmus wellesleybentonus Causey 1952: 171

FIGURES 7.30, 7.31

TYPE DEPOSITORY. Philadelphia Academy of Sciences.
TYPE LOCALITY. Arkansas: Phillips County; Helena.
DISTRIBUTION. Known only from the type locality.

FIG. 7.30. Distribution of *Eurymerodesmus wellesleybentonus.*

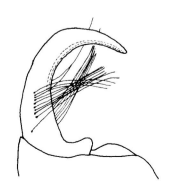

FIG. 7.31. *Eurymerodesmus welles-leybentonus:* Mesial view of telopodite of left gonopod (setae of dorsal row and prefemur omitted). *Redrawn from Causey 1952.*

Paresmus columbus Causey 1950: 272

FIGURES 7.32, 7.33

There are four additional species in the genus: two from type localities in Arkansas and one each from Louisiana and Texas. The distribution of the members of this genus indicate that they occur in lowland areas in the flood plain of the Gulf Coast.

TYPE DEPOSITORY. Philadelphia Academy of Sciences.
TYPE LOCALITY. Arkansas: Columbia County; Magnolia.
DISTRIBUTION. Known only from the type locality.

FIG. 7.32. Distribution of *Paresmus columbus.*

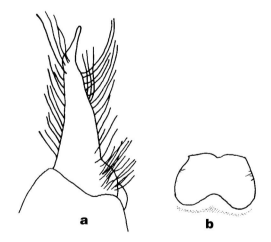

a
b

FIG. 7.33. *Paresmus columbus:* a, ventral view of right gonopod; b, ventral view of gonopodal opening (gonopods omitted). *Redrawn from Causey 1950.*

Paresmus polkensis Causey 1952: 5

FIGURE 7.34

TYPE DEPOSITORY. American Museum of Natural History.
TYPE LOCALITY. Arkansas: Polk County; 11 mi. N of Mena.
DISTRIBUTION. Known only from the type locality.

FIG. 7.34. Distribution of *Paresmus polkensis.*

Paresmus pulaski Causey 1950: 271

FIGURES 7.35, 7.36

TYPE DEPOSITORY. Philadelphia Academy of Sciences.
TYPE LOCALITY. Arkansas: Pulaski County; Sweet Home.
DISTRIBUTION. Arkansas: Grant, Pulaski.

FIG. 7.35. Distribution of *Paresmus pulaski.*

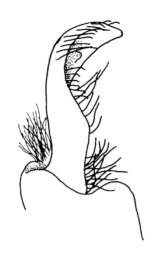

FIG. 7.36. *Paresmus pulaski*: Ventro-lateral view of right gonopod. *Redrawn from Causey 1950.*

Order Chordeumida

Family Cleidogonidae

Cleidogona arkansana Causey 1954: 66

FIGURES 7.37, 7.38

There are about twenty-five species in the genus *Cleidogona*, seventeen of which occur in North America.

TYPE DEPOSITORY. American Museum of Natural History.
TYPE LOCALITY. Arkansas: Dallas County; 4 mi. E of Princeton at picnic site on Rt. 8. Date: 7 January 1954.
DISTRIBUTION. Known only from the type locality.

FIG. 7.37. Distribution of *Cleidogona arkansana.*

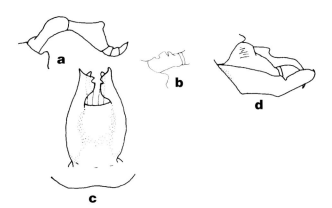

FIG. 7.38. *Cleidogona arkansana*: a, ninth leg; b, base of eleventh leg; c, ventral view of gonopod; d, lateral view of left gonopod. *Redrawn from Causey 1954.*

Cleidogona aspera Causey 1951: 78

FIGURES 7.39, 7.40

TYPE DEPOSITORY. Philadelphia Academy of Sciences.
TYPE LOCALITY. Arkansas: Lawrence County; 6 mi. E of Imboden.
DISTRIBUTION. Arkansas: Dallas, Lawrence, Randolph.

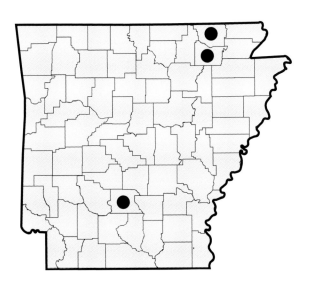

FIG. 7.39. Distribution of *Cleidogona aspera.*

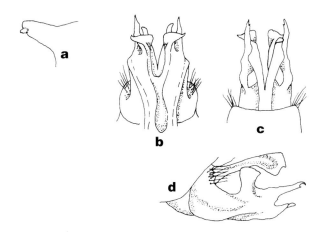

FIG. 7.40. Anatomical characteristics used to identify *Cleidogona aspera*: a, lateral view of sternal process at base of twelfth legs; b, ventral view of gonopods; c, dorsal view of gonopods; d, lateral view of left gonopod. *Redrawn from Causey 1951.*

Ofcookogona alia Causey 1951: 121

FIGURE 7.41, 7.42

There are two species in this genus, and both are described from Arkansas by Causey (1951). This species, *O. alia*, was collected from a pine and hardwood forest.

TYPE DEPOSITORY. Philadelphia Academy of Sciences.
TYPE LOCALITY. Arkansas: Union County; Junction City. Date: 25 December 1950.
DISTRIBUTION. Known only from the type locality.

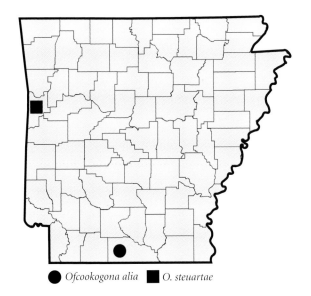

● *Ofcookogona alia*   ■ *O. steuartae*

FIG. 7.41. Distribution of *Ofcookogona alia* and *O. steuartae* .

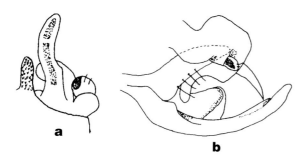

FIG. 7.42. *Ofcookogona alia*: a, sternal peg; b, gonopod, lateral view; c, gonopod, dorsal view. *Redrawn from Causey 1951.*

Ofcookogona steuartae Causey 1951: 121

FIGURES 7.41, 7.43

TYPE DEPOSITORY. Philadelphia Academy of Sciences.
TYPE LOCALITY. Arkansas: Sebastian County; Greenwood. Date: 26 November 1950.
DISTRIBUTION. Known only from the type locality.

FIG. 7.43. *Ofcookogona steuartae*, gonopod. *Redrawn from Causey 1951.*

Ozarkogona glebosa Causey 1951: 82

FIGURE 7.44, 7.45

There are two species in the genus, and both are described from Arkansas by Causey.

TYPE DEPOSITORY. Philadelphia Academy of Sciences.
TYPE LOCALITY. Arkansas: Washington County; Fayetteville.
DISTRIBUTION. Benton, Johnson, Washington.

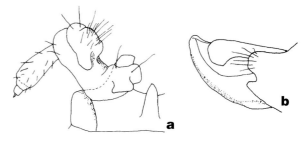

FIG. 7.45. Anatomical characteristics useful in identifying *Ozarkogona glebosa*: a, cephalic view of ninth leg and sternum; b, lateral view of right gonopod. *Redrawn from Causey 1951.*

Ozarkogona ladymani Causey 1952: 114

FIGURES 7.46, 7.47

TYPE DEPOSITORY. United States National Museum.
TYPE LOCALITY. Arkansas: Clay County; Rector.
DISTRIBUTION. Known only from the type locality.

FIG. 7.46. Distribution of *Ozarkogona ladymani*.

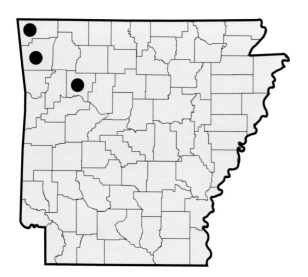

FIG. 7.44. Distribution of *Ozarkogona glebosa*.

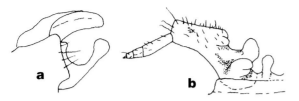

FIG. 7.47. Anatomical characteristics useful in identifying *Ozarkogona ladymani*: a, lateral view of right anterior gonopod; b, cephalic view of left posterior gonopod. *Redrawn from Causey 1952.*

Tiganogona moesta Causey 1951: 82

FIGURE 7.48, 7.49

There are two species in the genus *Tiganogona*, and both are endemic to the Interior Highlands. *Tiganogona brownae* Chamberlin, the second species in the genus, is known from one locality in St. Louis County in Missouri. The type locality of the Arkansas species, Blue Springs, has been developed into a tourist attraction west of Eureka Springs on Highway 62. TYPE DEPOSITORY. Philadelphia Academy of Sciences. TYPE LOCALITY. Arkansas: Carroll County; Blue Springs. DISTRIBUTION. Arkansas: Carroll, Washington.

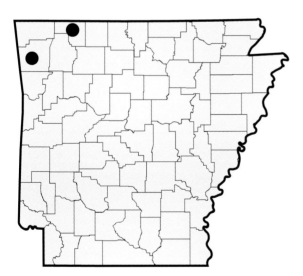

FIG. 7.48. Distribution of *Tiganogona moesta*.

FIG. 7.49. Anatomical characteristics useful in identifying *Tiganogona moesta*: a, caudal view of ninth leg and end of dorsal branch of gonopod; b, lateral view of right gonopod and ninth leg. *Redrawn from Causey 1951.*

Family Conotylidae

Trigenotyla parca Causey 1951: 118

FIGURES 7.50, 7.51

This is a monotypic genus described by Causey (1951) and known only from northwest Arkansas. Additional specimens have been collected in Washington County, adjacent to the type locality.

TYPE DEPOSITORY. Philadelphia Academy of Sciences.
TYPE LOCALITY. Arkansas: Carroll County; Blue Springs.
DISTRIBUTION. Arkansas: Carroll, Washington.

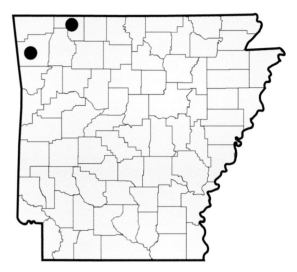

FIG. 7.50. Distribution of *Trigenotyla parca*.

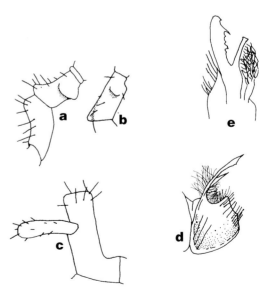

FIG. 7.51. Anatomical characteristics useful in identifying *Trigenotyla parca*: a, segments 2, 3, 4 of sixth leg; b, segment 4 of seventh leg; c, caudal view of right ninth leg; d, ventral view of right gonopod; e, lateral view of right gonopod. *Redrawn from Causey 1951.*

Craspedosoma flavidum Bollman 1888: 2

FIGURE 7.52

Bollman (1888) described several species in the genus *Craspedosoma*. When studied by other workers, most of these species are synonymized or transferred to the genus *Branneria*. Unfortunately, the types of *C. flavidum* have been lost, and further action must await the collection of additional material that can be referred to this species.

TYPE DEPOSITORY. United States National Museum (lost?).
TYPE LOCALITY. Arkansas: Clark County; Okolona.
DISTRIBUTION. Known only from the type locality.

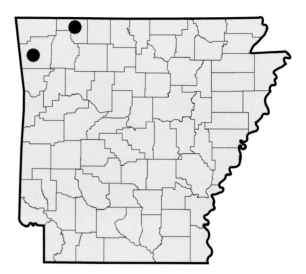

FIG. 7.53. Distribution of *Aliulus carrollus*.

FIG. 7.52. Distribution of *Craspedosoma flavidum*.

Order Julida

Family Paraiulidae

Aliulus carrollus Causey 1950: 45

FIGURES 7.53, 7.54

There are two other species in the genus: *A. caddoensis* from Oklahoma and *A. rugosus* from Pennsylvania, Ohio, Indiana, and Illinois. The type locality of *A. carrollus* is Blue Springs, now a commercial tourist area. Specimens of the species have also been collected in Washington County, adjacent to the type locality county.

TYPE DEPOSITORY. Philadelphia Academy of Sciences.
TYPE LOCALITY. Arkansas: Carroll County; Blue Springs.
DISTRIBUTION. Arkansas: Carroll, Washington.

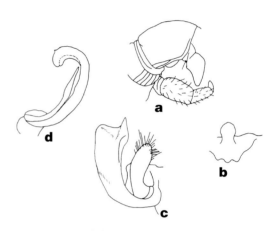

FIG. 7.54. Anatomical characteristics useful in identifying *Aliulus carrollus*: a, right side of anterior end of male; b, sternite of segment 8 of male; c, ectal view of left anterior gonopod; d, ectal view of left posterior gonopod. *Redrawn from Causey 1950.*

Okliulus beveli Causey 1953: 152

FIGURES 7.55, 7.56

The genus *Okliulus* was described by Causey (1953) from two species from Arkansas and Oklahoma. The second species in the genus, *O. carpenteri* Causey, is known from Latimer County, Oklahoma. Latimer County is in the heart of the Ozark Mountains, while Union County, Arkansas (type locality of *O. beveli*) is in the coastal flood plain.

TYPE DEPOSITORY. American Museum of Natural History.
TYPE LOCALITY. Arkansas: Union County; Junction City.
DISTRIBUTION. Known only from the type locality.

FIG. 7.55. Distribution of *Okliulus beveli*.

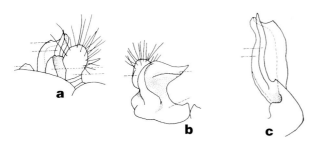

FIG. 7.56. *Okliulus beveli*: a, lateral view of left gonopods in situ; b, caudal view of right anterior gonopod; c, lateral view of right posterior gonopod. *Redrawn from Causey 1953.*

Oriulus grayi Causey 1950: 50

FIGURES 7.57, 7.58

The genus *Oriulus* contains eight additional species ranging throughout eastern North America with one

FIG. 7.57. Distribution of *Oriulus grayi*.

species reaching as far west as Colorado and Utah. The Arkansas endemic species occurs in the coastal flood plain in the vicinity of the White River.

TYPE DEPOSITORY. Philadelphia Academy of Sciences.
TYPE LOCALITY. Arkansas: Prairie County; De Valls Bluff.
DISTRIBUTION. Known only from the type locality.

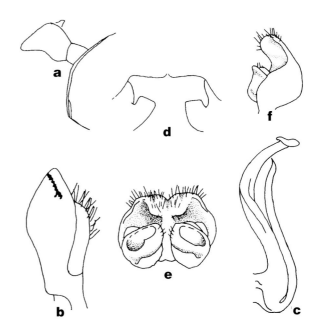

FIG. 7.58. *Oriulus grayi*: a, left side of anterior end of male; b, rectal view of left anterior gonopod; c, medial view of left posterior gonopod; d, ventral view of segment 3 of female, genital apparatus removed; e, caudal view of genital apparatus of female; f, lateral view of genital apparatus of female. *Redrawn from Causey 1950.*

Order Cambalida

Family Cambalidae

Cambala arkansana Chamberlin 1942: 3

FIGURE 7.59

The type locality of this species is in the coastal flood plain just south of the Ozark Mountain area. There are several species of animals whose distributions seem to be along the narrow border between the Ozark Mountains and the coastal flood plains. A great deal of additional collecting data will be necessary before we can determine if these species are residents of one or the other or both of these physiographic areas. There are ten additional species in the genus, and all of them occur in eastern North America.

TYPE DEPOSITORY. R. V. Chamberlin Collection.
TYPE LOCALITY. Arkansas: Randolph County;
Pocahontas.
DISTRIBUTION. Known only from the type locality.

FIG. 7.60. Distribution of *Polyzonium bikermani.*

FIG. 7.59. Distribution of *Cambala arkansana.*

Order Polyzoniida

Family Polyzoniidae

Polyzonium bikermani Causey 1951: 138

FIGURES 7.60, 7.61

There are two additional eastern North American species in the genus *Polyzonium.* Devil's Den State Park is the only known locality in the Ozark Mountains for *Polyzonium bikermani.* The park is also the type locality for the Interior Highland endemic rove beetle *Derops divalis* Sanderson.

TYPE DEPOSITORY. Philadelphia Academy of Sciences.
TYPE LOCALITY. Arkansas: Washington County; Devil's Den State Park.
DISTRIBUTION. Known only from the type locality.

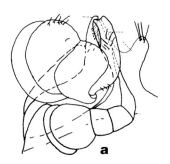
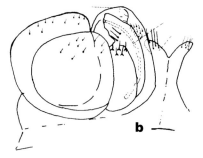

FIG. 7.61. Anatomical characteristics useful in identifying *Polyzonium bikermani*: a, posterior view of right gonopods and sternal horns; b, articles of anterior gonopod, 1–6. *Redrawn from Causey 1951.*

8

Class Arachnida

Arachnids

The class Arachnida includes a large and diverse number of organisms including the spiders, mites, ticks, scorpions, whipscorpions, short-tailed whipscorpions, whipspiders, ricinuleids, harvestmen, windscorpions, and pseudoscorpions. Only one of these groups, the pseudoscorpions, is known to have species that are endemic to Arkansas. The arachnids of the Interior Highlands are not well known and further study will probably lead to the discovery of additional new endemic forms.

Order Pseudoscorpiones— Pseudoscorpions

Family Neobisiidae

Microcreagris ozarkensis Hoff 1945: 34
FIGURES 8.1, 8.2

This Arkansas endemic is based on specimens that were collected in "leaf debris" from two localities in Washington County. The specimens were collected by M. W. Sanderson. The genus *Microcreagris* contains over twenty species known from North America, but it is uncertain which of these species is the closest relative of *M. ozarkensis*.

TYPE DEPOSITORY. Holotype and paratypes: Illinois Natural History Survey.
TYPE LOCALITY. Arkansas: Washington, Devil's Den State Park.
DISTRIBUTION. Known from the type locality and one additional locality near the town of Farmington, also in Washington County.

FIG. 8.1. Known distribution of *Microcreagris ozarkensis.*

Family Chernetidae

Pseudozaona occidentalis Hoff and Bolsterli 1956: 170
FIGURES 8.3, 8.4

This species was described from specimens collected in Fincher Cave and Carrol Cave in Washington County. Another Arkansas endemic species, a beetle *Rhadine ozarkensis,* was also described from specimens collected in Fincher Cave. Hoff and Bolsterli (1956) note that the genus *Pseudozaona* is known to contain only three additional species, one each from Costa Rica, Mexico, and Kentucky. The endemic Arkansas *Pseudozaona occidentalis* appears to be most closely related to *P. mirabilis* from Kentucky but can be separated from that species by "the somewhat smaller size and stouter nature of the palpal podomeres."

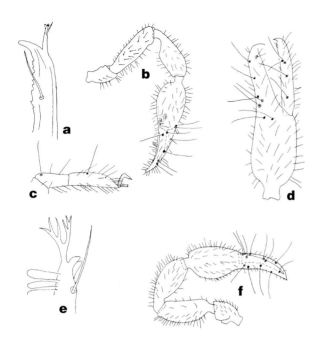

FIG. 8.3. Known distribution of *Pseudozaona occidentalis*.

FIG. 8.2. *Microcreagris ozarkensis:* a, Distal half of movable finger of chelicera; b, palp, male, dorsal; c, tarsus and metatarsus of fourth leg, male; d, external view of chela; e, galea and terminal portion of movable finger of chelicera; f, paplus, female, dorsal. *Redrawn from Hoff 1945.*

TYPE DEPOSITORY. Holotype and some paratypes: Illinois Natural History Survey.

TYPE LOCALITY. Arkansas: Washington, Fincher Cave.

DISTRIBUTION. Known only from the two caves from which the type material was collected in Washington County, Arkansas.

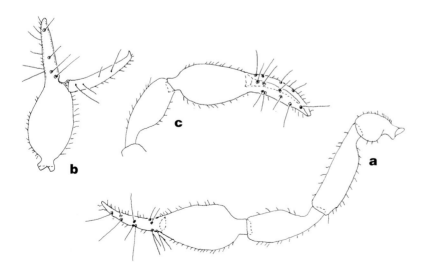

FIG. 8.4. *Pseudozaona occidentalis:* a, lateral view of Chela; b, palpal tibia and chela; c, palp, dorsal. *Redrawn from Hoff 1956.*

9

Class Insecta

Insects

The insects are the most successful group of organisms inhabiting the earth today. They live in almost every conceivable habitat from the Antarctic to the boiling hot springs of the desert southwest in North America. There have been over one million species described during the past two hundred years. The total number of species on the earth has been estimated to be as high as ten to thirty million. In Arkansas, we estimate that there may be thirty-five to forty thousand species. Most of these species are common and occur over a large geographical area. There are, however, a number of species that occur only in our state. This number of known Arkansas endemics increases as we study the Arkansas fauna in greater detail.

Order Diplura—Diplurans

Relatively little is known about Diplura in North America, and descriptions of species in this order have been sporadically published. A series of papers written by Smith from 1959 through 1969 recorded a number of new taxa in the family Japygidae, mostly from California. New North American species in the dipluran family Campodeidae have been described by Conde and Thomas (1957), Bareth, and Conde (1958), Conde and Geeraert (1962), and Conde (1973). Allen (1988b, 1993, 1994) has described three new species and one new genus from the mountains of western Arkansas.

The Diplura are of special significance because they stand at the base of the evolutionary tree to the class Insecta. The members of the order seem to retain many of the ancestral characteristics associated with more primitive classes in the phylum Arthropoda. Some of these characteristics include rudimentary appendages on the abdominal segments and spiracles on the thoracic segments in some families.

The preliminary data indicates that the Ozark/Ouachita Diplura represent a unique endemic fauna. Part of this fauna may have been isolated for at least 150 million years.

Family Japygidae

Catajapyx ewingi Fox 1941: 28

FIGURES 9.1, 9.2

Reddell (1983) noted that the genus *Catajapyx* was known from several countries in Europe. He also says, "The species listed below *[C. ewingi]* from Arkansas certainly does not belong in this genus." Specimens that could be identified as this species have not been collected since the original material was found in 1941. Further study of the exact placement and cladistic relationships will have to await the collection of additional material.

TYPE DEPOSITORY. Holotype and paratypes: United States National Museum.
TYPE LOCALITY. Arkansas: Howard County; near Hope.
DISTRIBUTION. Known only from the type locality.

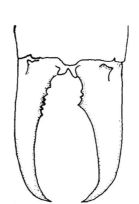

FIG. 9.1. Caudal cerci of *Catajapyx ewingi*. Redrawn from Fox 1941.

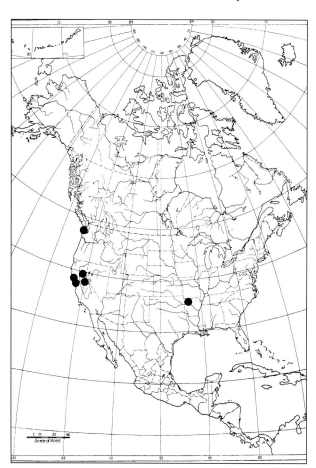

FIG. 9.2. Distribution of Diplura species endemic to Arkansas.

Occasjapyx carltoni Allen 1988: 22

FIGURES 9.2, 9.3, 9.4, 9.5

The genus *Occasjapyx* contains four west coast species in addition to the two endemic Arkansas species. The

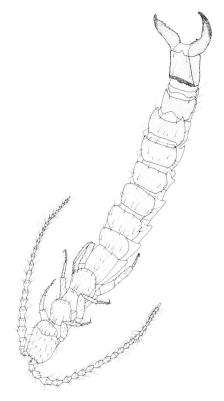

FIG. 9.4. *Occasjapyx carltoni* has been found at only one locality on a tributary of the Buffalo River in Newton County, Arkansas.

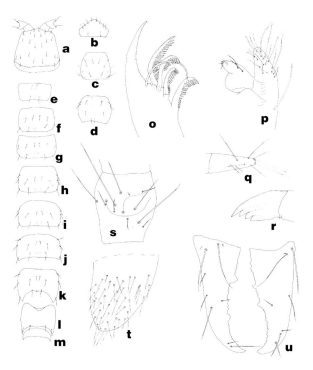

FIG. 9.5. *Occasjapyx carltoni*: a–i, dorsal surface showing position and number of major (M) setae on segments; a, head; b, pronotum; c, mesonotum; d, metanotum; e–m, abdominal segments 1–9; o, lacinia; p, galea; q, labial palpi; r, mandible; s, antennal segment 4; t, male lateral papillae; u, terminal abdominal cerci. *From Allen 1988b.*

FIG. 9.3. Distribution of the genus *Occasjapyx* in North America.

characteristics given by Smith (1959) seem to be distinct, thus, placement of the Arkansas species seems correct (Allen 1988b). Unlike many other endemic Arkansas taxa that have their nearest relatives in the east, *O. carltoni* shows western North American affinities.

TYPE DEPOSITORY. Holotype: American Museum of Natural History. Paratype: University of Arkansas Insect Collection.
TYPE LOCALITY. Arkansas: Newton. Date: 7 March 1988. Collector: C. E. Carlton.
DISTRIBUTION. Known only from the type locality.

Podocampa inveterata Allen 1993: 329

FIGURES 9.6, 9.7, 9.8

The genus *Podocampa* in the United States is known from five species in southwest Texas and in Louisiana. *Podocampa inveterata*, which is presently known only from Magazine Mountain in Logan County is the most northern record of this genus. The genus does occur in Cuba (one species) and several species are also found in southern Europe. The Arkansas species is readily recognized from other U.S. species by the presence of the bacilliform sensillum (bs) on the dorsum of antennal segment 3 (fig. 9.7) between phaneres b and c, and the presence of median anterior macrochaetae on abdominal segments 1–7 (fig. 9.8).

TYPE DEPOSITORY. Holotype: American Museum of Natural History. Paratype: American Museum of Natural History and the University of Arkansas Insect Collection.
TYPE LOCALITY. Arkansas: Logan County, Magazine Mountain.
DISTRIBUTION. Known only from the type locality.

FIG. 9.6. Distribution of *Podocampa inveterata* in Arkansas.

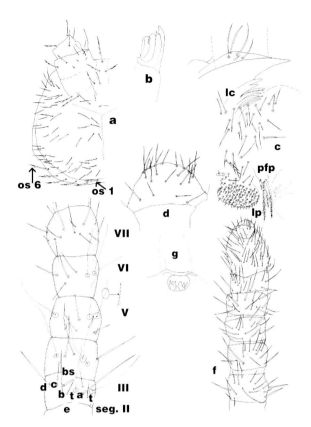

FIG. 9.7. *Podocampa inveterata*: a, Head, left side, dorsal; b, mandible; c, mouthparts, relative position, ventral; d, labrum; e, antennal segments 2–7; f, terminal antennal segment; g, cupiliform structure at apex of terminal antennal segment. os, occipital setae; lc, lacinia; lps, labial palps sensory seta; pfp, palpiform process; bs, bacilliform sensillum; t, trichobthria; a–d, antennal phaneres on segment 2. *From Allen 1993.*

Clivocampa solus Allen 1994: 375

FIGURES 9. 9, 9.10, 9.11

The genus *Clivocampa* and the type species of the genus, *solus*, are currently known only from Magazine Mountain in Logan County. The genus is closely related to *Podocampa*. *Clivocampa solus* and *Podocampa inveterata* are often found in the same microhabitats (i.e., under rocks the north-facing slope of Magazine Mountain). The genus *Clivocampa* is distinguished from *Podocampa* by two characters: (1) the presence of 4 + 4 and 6 + 6 lateral, posterior macrochaetae on abdominal segments 8 and 9, respectively (fig. 9.10); and (2) the baciliform sensillum on antennal segment 3 inserted laterally or ventrally between phaneres c and d (fig. 9.11).

TYPE DEPOSITORY. Holotype: American Museum of Natural History. Paratypes: American Museum of Natural History and the University of Arkansas Insect collection.
TYPE LOCALITY. Arkansas: Logan, Magazine Mountain.
DISTRIBUTION. Known only from the type locality.

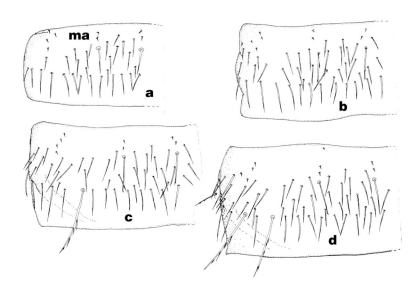

FIG. 9.8. *Podocampa inveterata:* a, abdominal tergite 1; ma, median anterior macrochaetae; b, tergite 2; c, tergite 3; d, tergite 4. *From Allen 1993.*

FIG. 9.9. Distribution of *Clivocampa solus* in Arkansas.

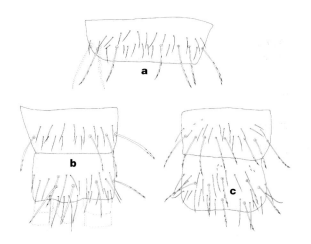

FIG. 9.11. *Clivocampa solus:* a, abdominal tergite 8; b, tergites 9, 10; c, sternites 9, 10. *From Allen 1994.*

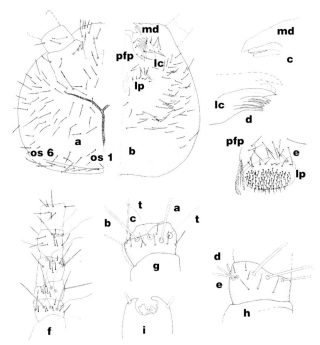

FIG. 9.10. *Clivocampa solus:* a, head, dorsal; b, head, ventral; c, mandible; d, lacinia; e, maxillary palp; f, antennal segments 3–7, dorsal; g, antennal segment 3, dorsal; h, antennal segment 3, ventral; i, apical segments with cupiliform organ. os, occipital setae; md, mandible; lc, lacinia, pfp, palpiform process; lp, labial palps; t, trichobothria; a–e, phaneres on antennal segment 3. *From Allen 1994.*

Order Ephemeroptera— Mayflies

Among the insect orders, the mayflies, or Ephemeroptera, exhibit two unique characteristics. Most of the life of a mayfly is spent as an aquatic larva. The larval stage may last from one to three years. After pupation in the aquatic environment, an adult emerges; however, this form is not quite an adult. The form that exits from the pupal case is called a subimago, because one additional molt, or shedding of the adult skin, is necessary before the sexually mature adult appears (fig. 9.12). Second, the imago and the sexually adult mayfly have vestigial mouth parts. The adults do not feed. The sole purpose of the adult is to mate and lay eggs for the next generation. Adult mayflies live for only one or two days. Among the some seventy species of mayflies found in Arkansas, two species appear to be endemic to the state.

● *Paraleptophlebia calcarica*
■ *Dannella provonshai*

FIG. 9.13. Distribution of mayflies, *Dannella*, endemic to Arkansas.

FIG. 9.12. Mayfly: subimago, molting. *Photograph by Gary Lantz.*

Family Ephemerellidae

Dannella provonshai McCafferty 1977: 886

FIGURES 9.13, 9.14, 9.15, 9.16, 9.17

Dannella provonshai is known from a single locality on the Mulberry River in Johnson County. McCafferty (1977) placed the species in the genus *Dannella*. This genus has two other members, *D. simplex* and *D. lita*, both confined to distributions east of the Mississippi River. McCafferty suggested that *provonshai* is most

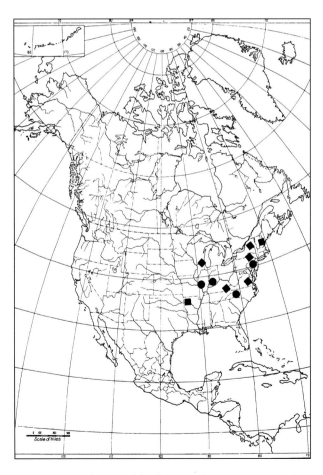

FIG. 9.14. Distribution of the three North American species in the genus *Dannella.*

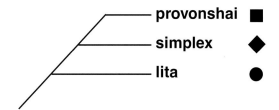

FIG. 9.15. Cladistic relationships of the three North American species in the genus *Dannella. From McCafferty 1977.*

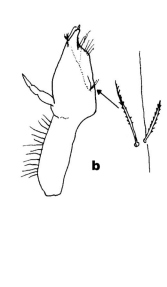

FIG. 9.17. Morphological characteristics used to identify *Dannella provonshai*: a, larval abdominal characters; b, enlarged medial setae of maxilla. *Redrawn from McCafferty 1977.*

closely related to *simplex*. Concerning the evolution of these taxa McCafferty said, "On the basis of the phylogeny of these species, it appears most likely that the species which gave rise to the sister species, *D. provonshai* and *D. simplex, . . .* was primarily Appalachian in distribution but ranged into the Ozark Plateau, possibly via the Illinois Ozarks or Cincinnati arch."

TYPE DEPOSITORY. Purdue University Insect Collection.
TYPE LOCALITY. Arkansas: Johnson County. Date: 2 June 1974.
Collectors: W. P. McCafferty, L. Dersch, A. V. Provonsha.
DISTRIBUTION. Known only from the type locality.

Family Leptophlebiidae

Paraleptophlebia calcarica Robotham and Allen 1988: 318

FIGURES 9.13, 9.18

This small mayfly species was collected from Gutter Rock Creek on the north slope of Magazine Mountain in 1986. Gutter Rock Creek is also the habitat of an endemic caddisfly, *Paucicalcarica ozarkensis* Mathis and Bowles. In the spring the creek flows rapidly but begins to dry in late June. By late June only a few standing pools remain, and by August there is only moist ground. Apparently, the stream life in this creek and similar creeks in the Interior Highlands have adapted to this seasonal occurrence of water.

The genus *Paraleptophlebia* contains about thirty-five species. Evolutionary relationships among the species have not been determined, but the sister species of *P. calcarica* appears to be *P. jeanae* Berner, which is known from the Appalachian Highlands and the coastal plain of Alabama.

TYPE DEPOSITORY. Holotype: American Museum of Natural History. Paratypes: University of Arkansas Insect Collection.
TYPE LOCALITY. Arkansas: Logan County; Gutter Rock Creek, Magazine Mtn. Date: 13 May 1986. Collector: David Bowles.
DISTRIBUTION. Known only from the type locality.

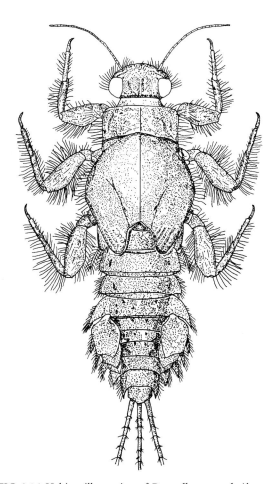

FIG. 9.16. Habitus illustration of *Dannella provonshai* larvae. *Redrawn from McCafferty 1977.*

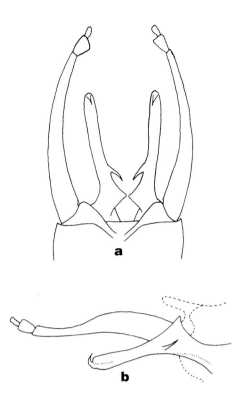

FIG. 9.18. Morphological characteristics used to identify *Paraleptophlebia calcarica*: a, ventral view of penis lobes and forceps; b, lateral view of left half of genitalia. *From Robotham and Allen 1988.*

Order Plecoptera—Stoneflies

Stoneflies are an aquatic group of insects found in most freshwater streams, lakes, and ponds. One genus, *Allocapnia*, has four species that are confined to the Highland areas of Arkansas, and the genus *Alloperla* has two Arkansas endemic species.

Species and sometimes genera within the stonefly order Plecoptera can be divided into those that inhabit clear, fast-flowing mountain streams and those that inhabit more sedate ponds or large rivers. Many of the species are sensitive to pollution and disturbance of their habitats. Dumping waste water into streams, building dams, and heavy silting caused by logging operations will invariably cause the elimination of stonefly species.

Family Capniidae—Genus Allocapnia

Allocapnia, winter stoneflies, are probably one of the most thoroughly collected insect taxa in North America. The adults emerge from November through March, thus the common name winter stonefly. They may be found on the concrete and stone pilings and abutments of bridges throughout most of eastern North America. Ross and Ricker intensively collected this genus throughout eastern North America, including Arkansas, during the sixties. Ross and Ricker (1971) had over one hundred people sending in winter stoneflies. This group of people were called "the winter stonefly club."

There are seven species that are endemic to the Interior Highlands of Missouri, Arkansas, and Oklahoma. Of these seven species, three are found only in Arkansas.

Ross and Ricker (1971) discussed at length and in some detail their ideas concerning the evolution and speciation in *Allocapnia*. These authors suggested that speciation in the Interior Highlands, including Arkansas, was the result of dispersal into and out of the area at various times during the Pleistocene. Populations in the Interior Highlands became isolated from those in the east and northeast and, subsequently, speciation occurred in some lineages. The Illinois Ozarks were seen as a corridor with suitable habitats through which *Allocapnia* populations could move from east to west and from north to south.

Allocapnia warreni Ross and Yamamoto 1966: 265

FIGURES 9.19, 9.20

This species has not been collected since the original material was taken. Due to urbanization, the banks along Clear Creek have changed radically during the last twenty-eight years. In 1988 the city of Fayetteville began dumping treated sewage effluent into Clear

FIG. 9.19. Distribution of *Allocapnia warreni*.

Creek. It is doubtful this species has survived: *Allocapnia warreni* is another casualty to man's infamous progress.

TYPE DEPOSITORY. Holotype: Illinois Natural History Survey.
TYPE LOCALITY. Arkansas: Washington County. Date: 29 January 1962. Collector: L. O. Warren.
DISTRIBUTION. Known only from the type locality.

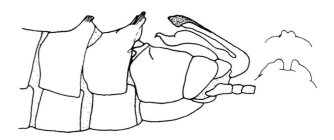

FIG. 9.22. The abdominal apical segments and genitalia of *Allocapnia ozarkana. Redrawn from Ross 1964.*

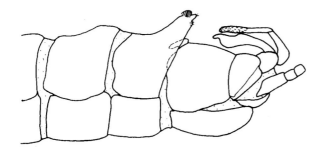

FIG. 9.20. The abdominal apical segments and genitalia of *Allocapnia warreni. Redrawn from Ross and Yamamoto 1966.*

Allocapnia ozarkana Ross 1964: 172

FIGURES 9.21, 9.22

TYPE DEPOSITORY. Holotype and paratypes: Illinois Natural History Survey.
TYPE LOCALITY. Arkansas: Madison County; Cannon Creek. Date: 26 January 1962. Collector: L. O. Warren.
DISTRIBUTION. Known only from type locality.

FIG. 9.21. Distribution of *Allocapnia ozarkana.*

Allocapnia oribata Poulton and Stewart 1987: 296

FIGURES 9.23, 9.24

This species is a good example of just how much work there is left to be done in Arkansas before we will be able to say with some certainty what the composition of the state's fauna may be. Even though Ross and Ricker (1971) had worked for several years collecting winter stoneflies in Arkansas, thirteen years after their paper was published yet another new species was discovered.

It is not clear which evolutionary group *A. oribata* belongs to. It is similar to a species named *A. malverna*, which was first discovered near Malvern, Arkansas, but also occurs in Louisiana. Poulton and Stewart (1987) give the following notes on the biology of the species: "The type males were collected on bridges from permanent, fourth order streams which have rock-rubble substrate. Large numbers of *A. mohri* Ross and Ricker, *A. rickeri* Frison, and *A. granulata* (Claassen) were also collected at these localities. Females of these species exhibit considerable variation in subgenital plate form; therefore we were unable to discern the female of *A. oribata.*"

FIG. 9.23. Distribution of *Allocapnia oribata.*

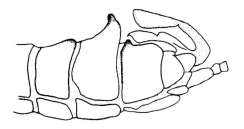 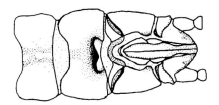

FIG. 9.24. The apical abdominal segments and genitalia of *Allocapnia oribata*. *Redrawn from Poulton and Stewart 1987.*

TYPE DEPOSITORY. Holotype: United States National Museum. Paratypes: North Texas State University Museum.

TYPE LOCALITY. Arkansas: Searcy County; Middle Fork of Little Red River, Hwy. 65 at Shirley. Date: 6 June 1985. Collector: B. C. Poulton.

DISTRIBUTION. Known only from the type locality.

Family Chloroperlidae

Alloperla ouachita Stark and Stewart 1983: 56
FIGURES 9.25, 9.26

There are five species in the genus *Alloperla* that occur in the Ozark/Ouachita Mountains: *A. leonarda, A. hamata, A. caudata* and (endemic to Arkansas) *A. ouachita* and *A. caddo* Poulton and Stewart. *Alloperla ouachita* has been collected only from the Little Missouri River in Montgomery County and, recently, from Big Hill Creek in Hot Spring County (Poulton and Stewart, pers. comm. 1991).

Stark et. al (1983) made the following comments on this species: "*A. ouachita* is a member of the *A. leonarda* complex which also includes *A. furcula* Surdick and *A. leonarda* and speciation is probably the result of isolation in the Ouachita Mountains of ancestral populations of *A. leonarda*."

TYPE DEPOSITORY. Holotype: United States National Museum. Paratypes: Brigham Young University, North Texas State University Museum.

TYPE LOCALITY. Arkansas: Montgomery County; Little Missouri River. Date: 20 June 1980. Collectors: E. J. Bacon and J. W. Feminella.

DISTRIBUTION. Arkansas: Hot Spring, Montgomery.

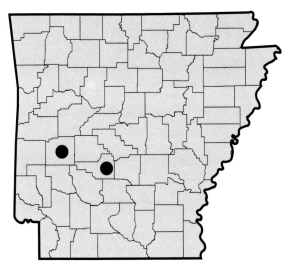

FIG. 9.25. Distribution of *Alloperla ouachita*.

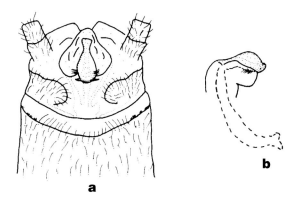

FIG. 9.26. Male genitalia of *Alloperla ouachita*. a, male dorsal aspect; b, lateral view of epiproct. *Redrawn from Stark and Stewart 1983.*

Alloperla caddo Poulton and Stewart 1987: 297

FIGURES 9.27, 9.28

Stark et al. (1983) published a key to the species of *Alloperla* found in the Ozark/Ouachita Mountain area. This represents an addition to that 1983 key. Poulton and Stewart (1987) have given a detailed analysis of this new species and the reader is referred to that paper for a complete discussion of *A. caddo*. Concerning the biology of this species, Poulton and Stewart say, "The type localities are all in the Ouachita Mountains and comprise first or second order, rock-rubble, intermittent streams. Adults were collected by sweeping riparian vegetation."

TYPE DEPOSITORY. Holotype: United States National Museum.
TYPE LOCALITY. Arkansas: Garland County; Middle Fork Saline River, Hwy. 7 at Iron Springs rec. area. Date: 6 June 1984. Collector: B. C. Poulton.
DISTRIBUTION. Arkansas: Garland, Perry.

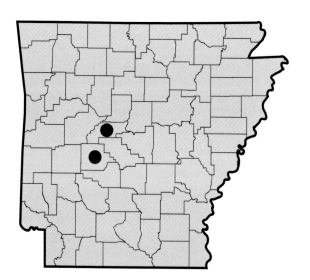

FIG. 9.27. Distribution of *Alloperla caddo*.

FIG. 9.28. *Alloperla caddo*: a, lateral view of tip of male epiproct; b, anterior view of tip of male epiproct; c, dorsal view of male genitalia; d, ventral view of female subgenital plate; e, lateral view of abdominal segments 7, 8, 9 of the female. *Redrawn from Poulton and Stewart 1987.*

Family Perlodidae

Isoperla szczytkoi Poulton and Stewart 1987: 298

FIGURES 9.29, 9.30

The genus *Isoperla* is widely distributed in North America and is also found in Europe, Japan, and northern China. The evolutionary relationships of the subgenera and the species have not been determined. Poulton and Stewart (1987) concluded that *I. szczytkoi* most closely resembles *I. decepta* Frison, also found in the Ozark/Ouachita Mountains.

I. szczytkoi has been collected only from Gutter Rock Creek on Magazine Mountain in Logan County. Two additional endemic insect species are also known only from Gutter Rock Creek.

TYPE DEPOSITORY. Holotype, allotype, and two nymphs: United States National Museum. Paratypes: North Texas State University Museum.

FIG. 9.29. Distribution of *Isoperla szczytkoi*.

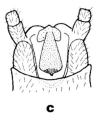
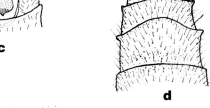
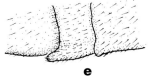

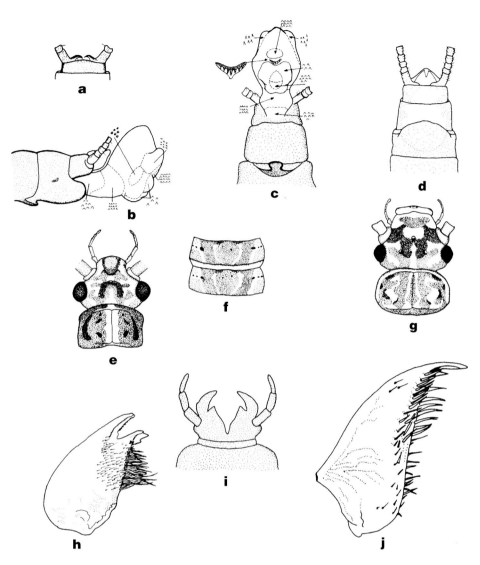

FIG. 9.30. *Isoperla szczytkoi*: a, dorsal male segment 1; b, male lateral terminalia; c, male ventral terminalia; d, female ventral terminalia; e, adult male head and pronotum; f, abdominal tergites of nymph; g, head and pronotum of nymph; h, right mandible of nymph; i, nymphal labium; j, right lacinia of nymph. *Redrawn from Poulton and Stewart 1987.*

TYPE LOCALITY. Arkansas: Logan County; Gutter Rock Creek, 33 km SE of Paris on side road near Hwy. 309. Date: 20 April 1985. Collector: B. C. Poulton. DISTRIBUTION. Known only from the type locality.

TYPE DEPOSITORY. Holotype: female.
TYPE LOCALITY. Arkansas: Polk County; Ouachita River. Collector: L. O. Warren. Date: 17 February 1962.
DISTRIBUTION. Arkansas: Polk, Scott.

Family Leuctridae

Zealeuctra wachita Ricker and Ross 1969: 1119

FIGURES 9.31, 9.32

Zealeuctra wachita is one of Arkansas's rarest endemics: only eight specimens have been collected. Besides the holotype (a female), Barry Poulton has recently collected five specimens. He collected one male and four females from the Ouachita River, 5.5 km west of Acorn, Polk County, and two additional specimens from Johnson Creek, 8 km west of Y City, Scott County (Poulton and Stewart, pers. comm. 1991).

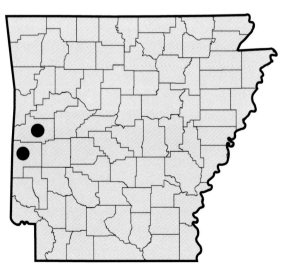

FIG. 9.31. Distribution of *Zealeuctra wachita*.

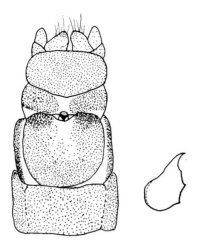

FIG. 9.32. The apical, abdominal segments, and female genitalia of *Zealeuctra wachita. Redrawn from Richer and Ross 1969.*

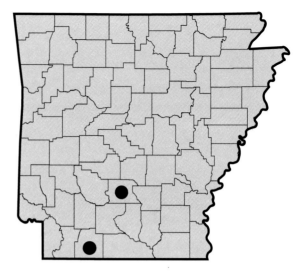

FIG. 9.33. Distribution of *Leuctra paleo.*

Leuctra paleo Poulton and Stewart 1991: 22

FIGURES 9.33, 9.34

This species occurs in "clear, sandy substrate, permanent streams in the Gulf Coastal Plain." It emerges in October. Two additional species in the genus, *L. richeri* and *L. tenuia*, also occur in the Interior Highlands (Poulton and Stewart 1991).

TYPE DEPOSITORY. Holotype: United States National Museum. Paratypes: United States National Museum; K. W. Stewart, North Texas State University.
TYPE LOCALITY. Arkansas: Columbia County; tributary of Smackover Creek at Hwy. 98, 8.8 km E of McNeil. Date: 3 October 1984. Collector: B. C. Poulton.
DISTRIBUTION. Arkansas: Dallas, Columbia.

Order Hemiptera

Family Tingidae

Acalypta susana Allen, Carlton, Tedder 1988: 126

Lace Bugs

FIGURES 9.35, 9.36

The genus *Acalypta* is found throughout North America and has been most recently studied by Drake and Lattin (1963). The cladistic affinities of the Arkansas endemic are uncertain.

FIG. 9.34. *Leuctra paleo:* a, male, terminal abdominal terga; b, male, terminalia, lateral view; c, male, terminalia, dorsal close-up of paraprocts and specilium; d, female, abdominal sterna. *Redrawn from Poulton and Stewart 1991.*

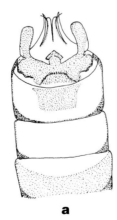

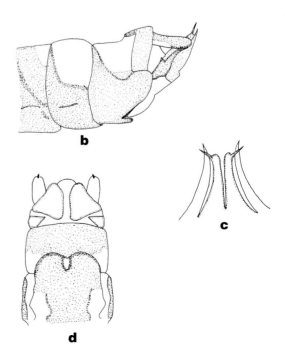

Allen et al. (1988) recorded the following biological notes about the paratype specimen collected by R. L. Leschen at Cove Lake on Magazine Mountain: "Following capture on 3 May, 1987, the Cove Lake paratype was placed on moist blotter paper in a petri dish with a small sample of moss-liverwort and as an alternative food source, a sample of slime mold, both collected from the log from which the specimen was taken. By 4 May the specimen had settled onto the moss and on the morning of 6 May was observed with stylets embedded in the axis of a moss branchlet. Observations were made under low indirect lighting. Even slight disturbances caused the specimen to withdraw the stylets and move to lower, darker locations in the sample. Subsequent to these observations the specimen was preserved." It should also be noted that Drake and Lattin (1963) said that members of the genus in North America were typically collected in association with mosses, and Bailey (1951) observed another species in the genus, *A. lillianus*, feeding on moss.

TYPE DEPOSITORY. Holotype: American Museum of Natural History. Paratype: University of Arkansas Insect Collection.

TYPE LOCALITY. Arkansas: Logan County; Magazine Mtn., NW slope, elev. 670 m. Date: 20 September 1987. Collector: S. A. Tedder.

DISTRIBUTION. Arkansas: Logan, Polk.

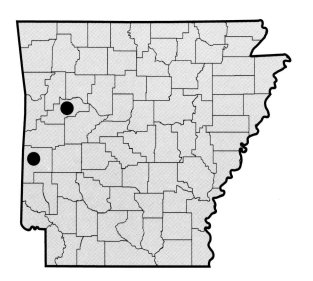

FIG. 9.35. Distribution of *Acalypta susana*.

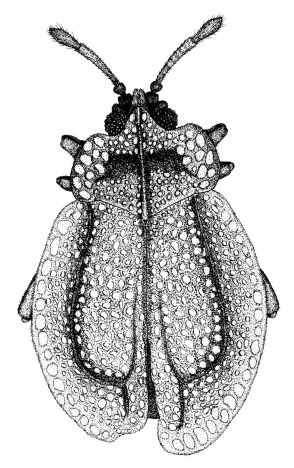

FIG. 9.36. General appearance and morphological characteristics used to identify specimens of *Acalypta susana. From Allen et al. 1988.*

Order Coleoptera—Beetles

The ground beetle family Carabidae is one of the larger groups of beetles. There are over forty thousand species worldwide and about three thousand species in North America. These species live in a variety of terrestrial habitats from lowland swamp areas to over twelve thousand feet elevation in the Rocky Mountains. Many of the species are predators, while other species feed on grass seeds or are scavengers. Some groups such as the *Pseudonapthalmus* and the *Rhadine*, which has one Arkansas endemic, inhabit caves and have lost their compound eyes and dark pigment as a result.

Two groups of ground beetles feed exclusively on snails. The Cychrini group is represented in Arkansas by two endemic species. Their heads and mandibles have become narrow and greatly elongated. This adaptation allows beetles such as the Arkansas endemic *Scaphinotus infletus* to push their heads into the shell openings of snails and consume the entire contents (figs. 9.37, 9.38, 9.39). The Licinini group (fig. 9.40) is common in Arkansas but does not appear to have any endemic species in the state. The Licinini have short heads and short, robust mandibles, and, therefore, cannot reach into snail shells; instead, the Licinini fillet the shell into halves (fig. 9.41) and eat the contents. These two beetle groups demonstrate remarkable adaptation for the utilization of a similar food resource.

FIG. 9.39. *Scaphinotus infletus* attacking a land snail. *Photograph by Robert T. Allen.*

FIG. 9.37. *Scaphinotus infletus*, a snail predator. *Photograph by Robert T. Allen.*

FIG. 9.40. A species of Licinini that feeds on land snails by cutting the shells in half. *Photograph by Robert T. Allen.*

FIG. 9.38. Land snails that are the food source for beetle species in the Cychrini and Licinini. *Photograph by Robert T. Allen.*

FIG. 9.41. Two halves of a land snail eaten by a Licinini. *Photograph by Robert T. Allen.*

TRIBE CYCHRINI

Scaphinotus (s. str.) *parisiana* Allen and Carlton 1988: 130

FIGURES 9.42, 9.43

Most species of Cychrini are found in mountainous areas in many parts of the world. It has not been possible to precisely determine the cladistic affinities of this species (Allen and Carlton 1988). However, the sister species appears to be *S. unicolor,* which is also found in the Interior Highlands.

TYPE DEPOSITORY. Holotype: American Museum of Natural History. Paratype: University of Arkansas Insect Collection.
TYPE LOCALITY. Arkansas: Logan County; Magazine Mtn.
DISTRIBUTION. Arkansas: Logan, Washington.

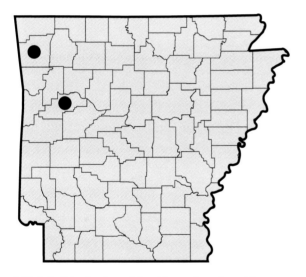

FIG. 9.42. Distribution of *Scaphinotus* (s. str.) *parisiana.*

Scaphinotus (Nomaretus) infletus Allen and Carlton 1988: 132

FIGURES 9.37, 9.39, 9.44, 9.45, 9.46, 9.47

There are five species in the subgenus *Nomaretus.* Four of these species occur west of the Mississippi River, while the fifth species, *S. bilobus,* occurs west of the Mississippi River and in previously glaciated areas in the east. The cladogram proposed by Allen and Carlton (1988) places *infletus* at the base of this monophyletic cluster of species.

Gidaspow (1973) notes that the subgenus "occurs in the Ozark Uplift (Missouri), except for *bilobus* which, following the retreating ice sheet, wandered to the region of the Great Lakes and the mountains of New York and New Hampshire." She also notes that *liebeki* occurs in the South in Texas and in one locality in Louisiana. It should also be noted that *fissicollis* and *cavicollis* are found well outside of the Interior Highlands in Kansas and that *cavicollis* is also found in Oklahoma. Because of the sympatry (overlapping distribution ranges) in these species, it is not possible to

FIG. 9.44. Distribution of *Scaphinotus* (*Nomaretus*) *infletus.*

FIG. 9.43. Lateral and dorsal views of the male genitalia of *Scaphinotus* (s. str.) *parisiana* used to identify specimens of this species. *From Allen and Carlton 1988.*

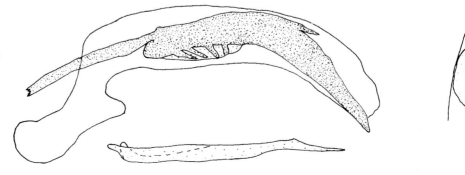

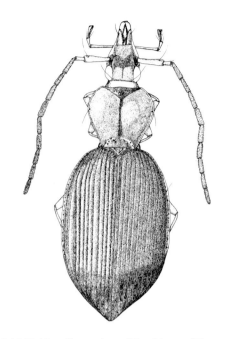

FIG. 9.45. Habitus illustration of *Scaphinotus (Nomaretus) infletus. Robert T. Allen.*

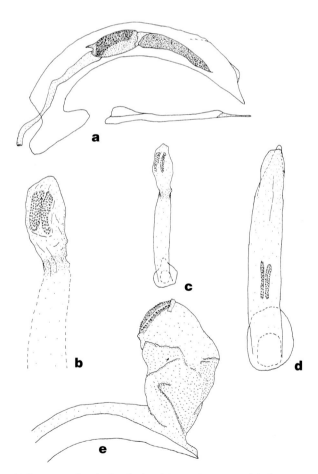

FIG. 9.46. Aedeagi of male *Scaphinotus (Nomaretus) infletus*: a, right lateral; b, enlarged internal sac everted, dorsal; c, dorsal internal sac everted distally, median lobe basally; d, dorsal internal sac not everted; e, right lateral internal sac everted. *From Allen and Carlton 1988.*

suggest what events may have led to their isolation and evolution.

TYPE DEPOSITORY. Holotype: American Museum of Natural History. Paratypes: University of Arkansas Insect Collection.

TYPE LOCALITY. Arkansas: Newton County; Natural Bridge rec. area.

DISTRIBUTION. Known only from the type locality.

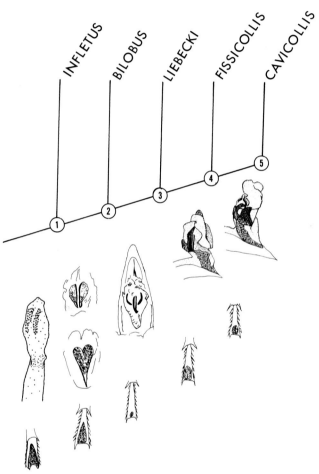

FIG. 9.47. A proposed cladogram of relationships among the five species in the subgenus *Nomaretus*. The top line of illustrations below the cladogram depicts changes in the armament on the internal sac of the male aedeagus. The bottom line of illustrations depicts changes in the squamous pads on the ventral surface of the male protarsi. *From Allen and Carlton 1988.* (See text for further discussion.)

TRIBE RHADINI

Rhadine ozarkensis Sanderson and Miller 1941: 39

FIGURE 9.48

This Arkansas endemic is apparently a cave species. Barr (1974) divided the sixty or so species of *Rhadine* into six species groups. *Rhadine ozarkensis* belongs to the *lavalis* group, which also includes *R. lavalis* LeConte, *R. caudata* LeConte, and *R. euprepes*. The cladistic relationships among the species are unclear, but Sanderson and Miller (1941) considered *R. ozarkensis* to be very similar to *R. caudata*.

TYPE DEPOSITORY. Holotype: Illinois Natural History Survey. Paratypes: Museum of Comparative Zoology, Harvard University; Snow Entomology Museum, University of Kansas.
TYPE LOCALITY. Arkansas: Washington County; Fincher Cave. Date: 20 January 1940. Collectors: M. W. Sanderson and A. Miller.
DISTRIBUTION. Known only from type locality.

FIG. 9.48. Distribution of *Rhadine ozarkensis*.

TRIBE PTEROSTICHINI

Evarthrus parasodalis Freitag 1969: 150

FIGURES 9.49, 9.50, 9.51, 9.52

This species is known only from the Ozark and Ouachita Mountains of Arkansas. Within the genus *Evarthrus,* the Arkansas endemic belongs to a distinct evolutionary lineage consisting of five species. The other species in the group (*E. furtivus, E. sodalis sodalis,* *E. sodalis colossus, E. sodalis lodingi*) all occur north and east of the range of *E. parasodalis*.

Members of the genus *Evarthrus* possess a curious, though not unique, adaptation involving the wings. In beetles, the elytra, the hard outer pair of wings, cover the membranous, the second pair of wings. When beetles fly, the elytra are held up and out from the body while the membranous wings propel the insect through the air. In *Evarthrus,* the membranous wings are greatly reduced or absent, thus, these species cannot fly. The elytra have become united along the midline and usually cannot be separated. The result is that *Evarthrus* are reduced to one form of locomotion—walking.

Evarthrus species, including the Arkansas endemic, are common on the forest floor. They may be predators or scavengers; they hide under rocks and logs by day and come out to feed at night.

TYPE DEPOSITORY. Holotype and allotype: Museum of Comparative Zoology, Harvard University. Paratypes: Cornell University, Illinois Natural History Survey, R. Freitag Collection, Ross T. Bell Collection, University of Alberta Strickland Museum, University of Arkansas Insect Collection.
TYPE LOCALITY. Arkansas: Washington County; forest leaf litter. Date: 16 July 1960. Collectors: Otis and Maxine Hite.
DISTRIBUTION. Arkansas: Conway, Franklin, Garland, Montgomery, Washington

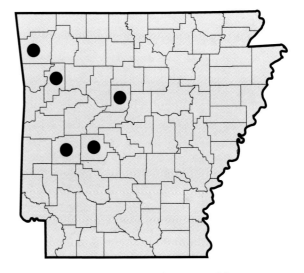

FIG. 9.49. Distribution of *Evarthrus parasodalis*.

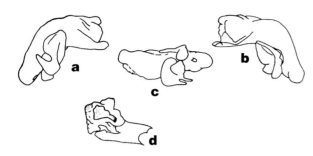

FIG. 9.50. The male genitalia used to identify specimens of *Evarthrus parasodalis*: a, right lateral; b, left lateral; c, ventral; d, dorsal, soc partially everted. *Redrawn from Freitag 1969.*

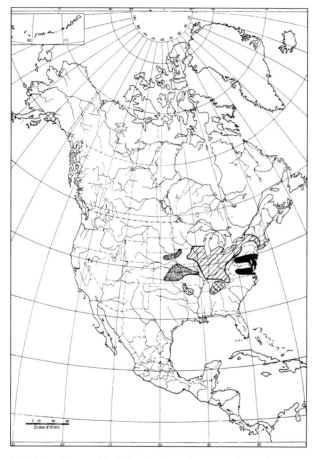

FIG. 9.51. Geographical distribution of species of *Evarthrus* closely related to *E. parasodalis*.

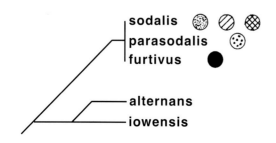

FIG. 9.52. Cladistic relationships of the *E. parasodalis* lineage. *Modified from Freitag 1969.*

Family Dytiscidae—Predaceous Diving Beetles

Hydroporus sulphurius Matta and Wolfe 1979: 289

FIGURES 9.53, 9.54

The genus *Hydroporus* is a large group with over one hundred known species found throughout the United States. Matta and Wolfe (1979) assigned this Arkansas endemic to the *pulcher* group in the genus. These authors state that "the aedeagus is distinct and may be used to separate this species from all others in the group."

TYPE DEPOSITORY. Holotype: United States National Museum, type number 95565. Paratypes: United States National Museum, Canadian National Collection and 13 retained by authors (6 by J. F. Matta and 7 by G. W. Wolfe).
TYPE LOCALITY. Arkansas: Benton; Sulphur Springs.
DISTRIBUTION. Known only from the type locality.

FIG. 9.53. Known distribution of *Hydroporus sulphurius*.

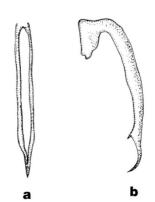

FIG. 9.54. *Hydroporus sulphurius*: Aedeagus: a, dorsal; b, lateral view. *Redrawn from Matta and Wolfe 1979.*

Family Pselaphidae—Short-Winged Mold Beetles

Short-winged mold beetles live among the leaf debris, rocks, and soil on the forest floor. Since most of the species are very small (less than 0.25 in. long), they are difficult to see and collect by hand. Beetle collectors take Berlese samples, a special collecting technique in which leaf debris, soil, and pieces of rotting logs are collected in the forest and placed in funnels. An incandescent lamp is suspended over the funnels. The heat from the lamp dries out the samples and causes the beetles to move downward into a jar of alcohol. Using this collection technique, entomologists may get hundreds of small insect specimens that belong to a variety of orders and families.

Short-winged mold beetles may be predators or scavengers. There are several hundred species in North America, but in tropical areas there appear to be thousands of species mostly undescribed and unnamed.

TRIBE BATRISINI

Arianops sandersoni Barr 1974: 21

FIGURES 9.55, 9.56, 9.57

M. W. Sanderson originally collected this species in 1949, but its formal description had to wait until 1974 when Thomas Barr of the University of Kentucky studied the genus *Arianops* thoroughly. At the time Barr did

his work, *A. sandersoni* was the only member of this genus found outside of the Appalachian Mountains, and this species was known only from one female specimen. In 1986 males of the species were collected from Bear Hollow on Magazine Mountain. These males, as well as another new species (*A. stephani*) in the genus from Latimer County, Oklahoma, were described by Carlton and Allen (1989). The existence of the genus *Arianops* no doubt indicates an ancient land connection with the Appalachian Mountains.

TYPE DEPOSITORY. Holotype: Illinois Natural History Survey.
TYPE LOCALITY. Arkansas: Logan County; Magazine Mtn. Collector: M. W. Sanderson.
DISTRIBUTION. Known only from type locality.

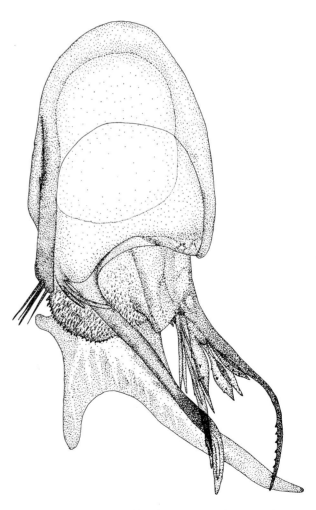

FIG. 9.56. The male genitalia of *Arianops sandersoni* used to identify specimens of this species. *From Carlton and Allen 1989.*

● *Arianops sandersoni*
■ *Ouachitychus parvoculus*

FIG. 9.55. Distribution of *Arianops sandersoni* and *Ouachitychus parvoculus.*

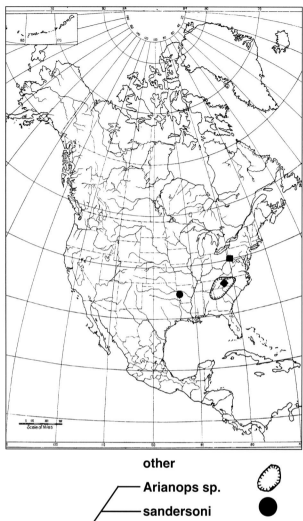

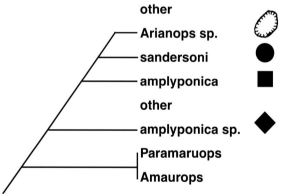

FIG. 9.57. Cladistic relationships and geographic distribution of species closely related to *Arianops sandersoni.*

Arianops copelandi Carlton 1990: 366

FIGURES 9.58, 9.59

Carlton and Allen (1989) mentioned the existence of a third species of *Arianops* present on Pinnacle Mountain in Pulaski County, Arkansas, but did not describe that species because only females were known. Carlton was later able to find males of the Pinnacle Mountain form in samples collected in 1988. Carlton and Cox (1990)

FIG. 9.58. Distribution of *Arianops copelandi.*

discussed the isolation and subsequent origin of the Ouachita Mountain *Arianops* and described the Pinnacle Mountain form as *A. copelandi.* As mentioned previously, over thirty species of *Arianops* are known from the Appalachian Mountains. The Ouachita Mountain fauna of *Arianops* now numbers three species. The distinct distribution of this genus between the Appalachians and the Ouachita Mountains is extremely interesting. Carlton and Cox (1990) suggest that a barrier existed between the southern Ouachita Mountain and the northern Ozark Mountains during the mid-Jurassic and Cretaceous periods. This barrier was a drainage basin that prevented flightless, soil-dwelling forms such as *Arianops* from moving into the northern areas. Much additional collecting in the Interior Highlands is needed to refute or confirm this hypothesis.

TYPE DEPOSITORY. Holotype: Field Museum of Natural History, Chicago. Paratypes: University of Arkansas Arthropod Museum; Donald S. Chandler Collection.
TYPE LOCALITY. Arkansas: Pulaski County; leaf litter at NE slope near summit of Pinnacle Mtn. Date: 15 April 1988. Collector: C. E. Carlton.
DISTRIBUTION. Known only from the type locality.

TRIBE TYCHINI

Ouachitychus parvoculus Chandler 1988: 160

FIGURES 9.55, 9.60, 9.61

Based on a single species, this endemic genus and species were collected in Bear Hollow on Magazine

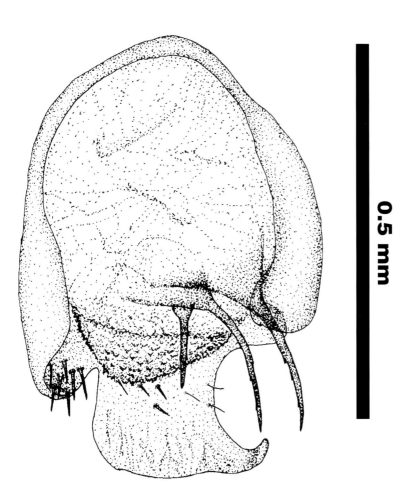

FIG. 9.59. *Arianops copelandi.* Aedeagus, dorsal aspect. *From Carlton and Cox 1990.*

0.5 mm

Mountain. The taxa were recognized and described by Don Chandler of the University of New Hampshire with material collected by S. A. Tedder. *Ouachitychus parvoculus* is similar in appearance to *Arianops sandersoni.* The existence and apparent confinement of *O. parvoculus* and *A. sandersoni* on Magazine Mountain is a most interesting phenomenon. The time at which they were isolated on the mountain is not well understood, nor are the reasons for their isolation. These species, as well as other Magazine Mountain endemics, may be as old as 150 million years.

TYPE DEPOSITORY. Holotype: Field Museum of Natural History, Chicago.

TYPE LOCALITY. Arkansas: Logan County; Magazine Mtn., 0.5 mi. S of Greenfield on E side of Hwy. 309. Date: 27 May 1987. Collector: S. A. Tedder.

DISTRIBUTION. Known only from the type locality.

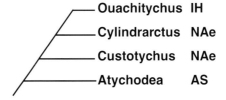

FIG. 9.61. Cladistic relationships of genera closely related to *Ouachitychus. From Chandler 1988.*

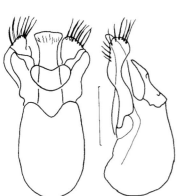

FIG. 9.60. The male genitalia of *Ouachitychus parvoculus* used to identify specimens of this species. *Redrawn from Chandler 1988.*

Family Chrysomelidae

Pachybrachis pinicola Rouse and Medvedev 1972: 82

Leaf Beetles

FIGURES 9.62, 9.63

TYPE DEPOSITORY. Unknown.
TYPE LOCALITY. Arkansas: Nevada County; on pine.
Date: 6 June 1962.
DISTRIBUTION. Known only from the type locality.

● *Pachybrachis pinicola*
■ *Lema maculicollis* ab. *inornata*

FIG. 9.62. Distribution of *Pachybrachis pinicola* and *Lema maculicollis* ab *inornata*.

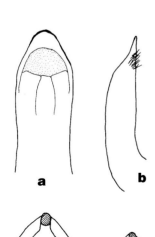

FIG. 9.63. The male genitalia (a, b) and claws of the fore and hind legs of the males (c,d) of *Pachybrachis pinicola* used to identify specimens. *Redrawn from Rouse and Medvedev 1972.*

Lema maculicollis ab. inornata Rouse and Medvedev 1972: 81

FIGURE 9.62

TYPE DEPOSITORY. Unknown.
TYPE LOCALITY. Arkansas: Montgomery County.
DISTRIBUTION. Arkansas: Logan, Montgomery.

Order Trichoptera—Caddisflies

The Trichoptera or caddisflies are a large and diverse group of aquatic insects. These insects play an important part in most freshwater ecosystems by helping break down detritus in the system and subsequently being consumed by larger invertebrates and vertebrates. Like the stoneflies, caddisflies are also ecologically sensitive. Pollution and disturbance of habitats will result in the extinction of caddisfly species.

Family Psychomyiidae

Paduniella nearctica Flint 1967: 310

FIGURES 9.64, 9.65

The description of *P. nearctica* in 1967 marked the first known occurrence of a member of the subfamily Paduniellinae from the Nearctic region. Bowles and Allen (1988) later described the female of the species. The genus *Paduniella* is found in Sri Lanka (Ceylon), Java, Africa, India, Philippines, Indonesia, and the south Ussuri River region in Russia. There are approximately twenty species in the genus. Flint (1967)

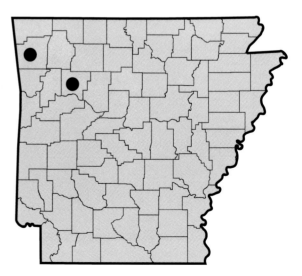

FIG. 9.64. Distribution of *Paduniella nearctica.*

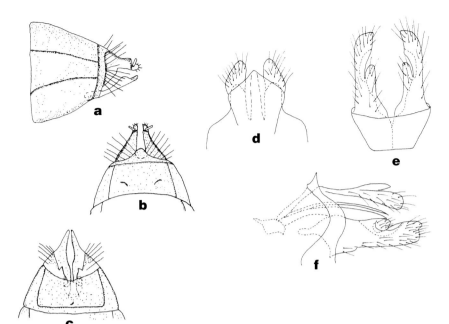

FIG. 9.65. a–f, female and male genitalia of *Paduniella nearctica:* a, female, lateral view; b, female, dorsal; c, female, ventral; d, male, 10th tergum and cerci, dorsal; e, male, claspers, ventral; f, male, genitalia, lateral view. *From Flint 1967; Bowles and Allen 1988.*

indicated that the Arkansas species appeared to be most closely related to *P. sangharvittra* Schmid from Ceylon.

The Arkansas Ozark's connection with the Far East is a particularly interesting geographic phenomenon. The connection indicates an ancient biotic connection between the Ozarks and the southern part of India, specifically Sri Lanka (Ceylon), that could be as old as 100 to 150 million years.

TYPE DEPOSITORY. Holotype: USNM 69201, United States National Museum. Paratypes: United States National Museum.

TYPE LOCALITY. Arkansas: Washington County; Devil's Den State Park. Date: 30 May 1966. Collector: R. W. Hodges.

DISTRIBUTION. Arkansas: Johnson, Washington.

FIG. 9.66. Distribution of *Paucicalcarica ozarkensis.*

Family Hydroptilidae

Paucicalcarica ozarkensis Matthis and Bowles 1989: 188

FIGURES 9.66, 9.67

This form represents an endemic genus and species in Arkansas. Two males of the species were collected from Gutter Rock Creek on Magazine Mountain. Although this creek has a heavy flow in the early spring, it rapidly dries to a series of intermittent small pools in late June and July. In May 1987, Richard Leschen collected with a black light the specimens representing this species. Repeated attempts to collect more specimens have not been successful. Another Arkansas endemic species, the

mayfly *(Paraleptophlebia calcarica)* is also known from Gutter Rock Creek.

TYPE DEPOSITORY. Holotype and paratype: United States National Museum.

TYPE LOCALITY. Arkansas: Logan County; Gutter Rock Creek on Magazine Mtn. near Paris. Collector: R. A. Leschen.

DISTRIBUTION. Known only from type locality.

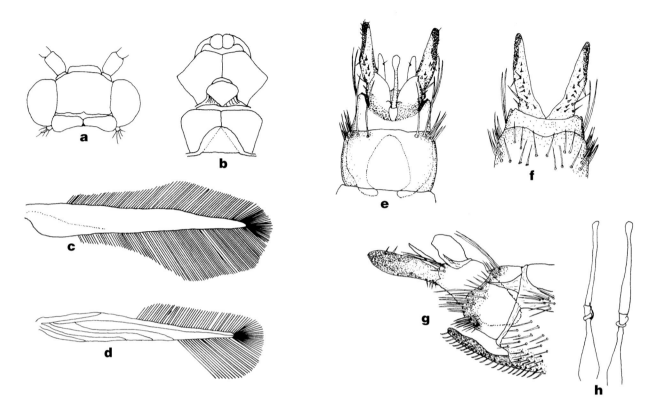

FIG. 9.67. Morphological characteristics used to identify *Paucicalcarica ozarkensis*: a, dorsal view of head; b, dorsal view of thorax; c, forewing; d, hindwing; e, dorsal view of male genitalia; f, ventral view of male genitalia; g, lateral view of male genitalia; h, lateral and dorsal views of aedeagus. *From Mathis and Bowles 1989.*

Ochrotrichia robisoni Frazer and Harris 1991: 364

FIGURE 9.68, 9.69

This is a second species of micro–caddisfly in the family Hydroptididae currently known from only one locality in Arkansas. Specimens of the species were collected by Henry Robison from Bear Creek in Perry County in 1983. The species belongs to the *Ochrotrichia shawnee* group, a distinct phylogenetic lineage consisting of seven other species. The closest relative of *O. robisoni* appears to be *O. contorta*, which is endemic to the Interior Highlands of Arkansas and Missouri. Another closely related species is *O. tuscaloosa*, known only from Alabama. Frazer and Harris (1991) published a cladogram depicting the relationships of the species in the *O. shawnee* complex. The cladogram, however, does not indicate what vicariant event might have isolated ancestral populations of *O. robisoni* and led to its subsequent evolution.

TYPE DEPOSITORY AND HOLOTYPE: United States National Museum. Paratypes: United States National Museum, Illinois Natural History Survey, University of Alabama Insect Collection, Southern Arkansas University

Museum, collections of K. S. Frazer and S. C. Harris.
TYPE LOCALITY. Arkansas: Perry County; Bear Creek at Hwy. 7, 2 mi. S of Hollis. Date: 11 June 1983. Collector: Henry W. Robison.
DISTRIBUTION. Known only from the type locality.

FIG. 9.68. Distribution of *Ochrotrichia robisoni.*

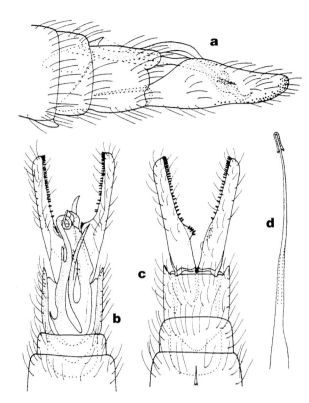

FIG. 9.69. Male genitalia of *Ochrotrichia robisoni*: a, lateral view; b, dorsal view; c, ventral view; d, phallus, dorsal view. *Redrawn from Frazer and Harris 1991.*

Family Glossosomatidae

Agapetus medicus Ross 1938: 107

FIGURES 9.70, 9.71

Although we have not been able to locate McFadden Springs, the original locality from which this species

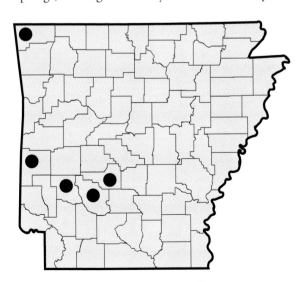

FIG. 9.70. Distribution of *Agapetus medicus.*

was collected, many additional specimens of the species have been collected from several Arkansas counties. The species is an inhabitant of cool swift-moving mountain streams. Evolutionary relationships within the genus *Agapetus* have not been worked out. We do not know what the nearest relative of *medicus* might be. There are several other species of *Agapetus* that occur in the Interior Highlands, but the Arkansas species is the only form endemic to the state.

TYPE DEPOSITORY. Holotype and paratypes: Illinois Natural History Survey.
TYPE LOCALITY. Arkansas: county unknown; McFadden Springs cannot be located on current maps.
DISTRIBUTION. Arkansas: Benton, Clark, Hot Spring, Pike, Polk.

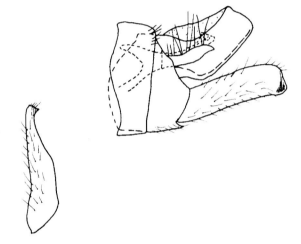

FIG. 9.71. The male genitalia used to identify specimens of *Agapetus medicus. Redrawn from Ross 1938.*

Family Helicopsychidae

Helicopsyche limnella Ross 1938: 179

FIGURES 9.72, 9.73

Ross (1959) discussed the distribution and some of the relationships of the North American *Helicopsyche* species. Ross notes that this is primarily a tropical or subtropical group with some species extending their range into the United States. Ross also considered *H. limnella* as "so close to *H. mexicana* morphologically that it is here [1959 paper] considered as merely an outpost colony of *mexicana*." Recent examination of the North American species in *Helicopsyche* has shown that the Arkansas *limnella* is definitely a good species (Bowles, pers. comm. 1988).

The close relationship of the Arkansas *H. limnella* populations with *H. mexicana*, found in Mexico, does show yet another very interesting distribution pattern. In this case we see that there is evidence that some Neotropical elements may have made a contribution to the Arkansas fauna.

TYPE DEPOSITORY. Holotype and paratypes: Illinois Natural History Survey.

TYPE LOCALITY. Arkansas: county unknown. Date: 5 June 1937. Collector: H. H. Ross.

DISTRIBUTION. Arkansas: Benton, Clark, Crawford, Franklin, Garland, Hot Spring, Johnson, Madison, Montgomery, Polk, Saline, Washington.

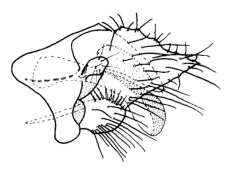

FIG. 9.73. The male genitalia of *Helicopsyche limnella* used to identify specimens. *Redrawn from Ross 1938.*

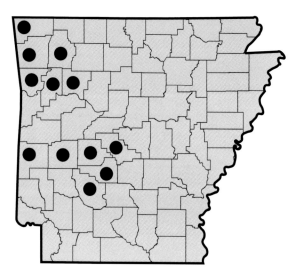

FIG. 9.72. Distribution of *Helicopsyche limnella*.

10

Class Osteichthyes

Bony Fishes

Fishes are the most successful and amazingly diverse group of vertebrate animals on earth; the number of living species is estimated to be anywhere from eighteen thousand to over forty thousand, depending upon the authority used. Fishes total more than half of all living vertebrate species. Tremendous variation in morphology, behavior, and ecology is exhibited by fishes. Members of the most advanced group, the Teleostei, have penetrated virtually every conceivable aquatic habitat, ranging from ocean depths of -11,000 m to mountain heights of 4,500 m and temperatures of 43° C in hot springs to -1.8° C in subfreezing water (Lagler et al. 1977).

In Arkansas we are fortunate to possess a wonderfully rich assortment of fishes. The state has 215 fish species, 197 of which are native and 18 that have been introduced to state waters (Robison and Buchanan 1988). Modern fishes are divided into three basic groups or classes: Chondrichthyes (sharks, skates, and rays), Agnatha (lampreys and hagfishes), and Osteichthyes (bony fishes). Of course, in Arkansas we have no chondrichthyian fishes; however, we do have four agnathan lampreys. The remaining 193 native species are bony fishes. Of these 193, 5 species (2 madtom catfishes and 3 darters) are endemic to the state waters.

Noturus lachneri Taylor 1969: 54

Ouachita Madtom

FIGURES 10.1, 10.2

The Ouachita madtom, brownish to gray in coloring, is a slender catfish with an adnate adipose fin, a terminal mouth, nearly equal jaws, and ten preoperculo-mandibular pores. A single internasal pore is present. This rare species differs from the tadpole madtom, *N. gyrinus*, because it has one internasal pore instead of

two and sixteen to eighteen anal rays instead of fourteen to sixteen. It differs from the slender madtom, *N. exilis* because of it lacks serrae on the pectoral spine, has more caudal rays, and typically has eight, rather than nine, pectoral rays (Robison and Buchanan 1988).

Generally, the Ouachita madtom occurs in the small- to moderate-sized gravel-bottomed streams of the Saline River system that are clear and high gradient. The madtom frequents quiet backwater areas with substrates varying in size from cobblestone-sized rocks to small gravel (Robison and Harp 1985). Occasional specimens have also been collected during the day in very shallow riffles under large rocks. Foods include primarily ephemeropterans, dipterans (Chironomidae), coleopterans, trichopterans, isopods, copepods, and gastropods. Robison and Buchanan (1988) hypothesized that perhaps *N. lachneri* seeks smaller tributaries for spawning during the summer period.

Noturus lachneri has been considered a "threatened"

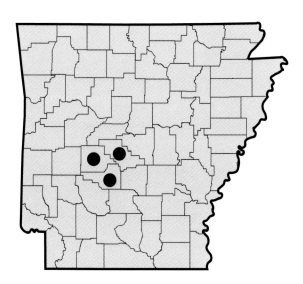

FIG. 10.1. Distribution of *Noturus lachneri*.

FIG. 10.2. *Noturus lachneri*, the Ouachita madtom, endemic to the Ouachita Mountains of Arkansas. *Photograph by Henry W. Robison.*

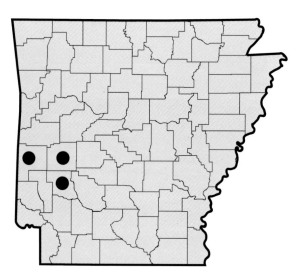

FIG. 10.3. Distribution of *Noturus taylori*.

fish species in the state because of multiple complex environmental threats to its continued existence, which were coupled with the combination of a relatively small population size and sporadic and restricted distribution.

TYPE DEPOSITORY. Holotype: USNM 201592, United States National Museum.
TYPE LOCALITY. Arkansas: Middle Fork Saline River; Hwy. 7, 11.2 mi. N of Mountain Valley, Garland County. Date: 27 May 1967. Collectors: L. and B. Knapp.
DISTRIBUTION. Arkansas: Garland, Hot Spring, Saline

Noturus taylori Douglas 1972: 785

Caddo Madtom

FIGURES 10.3, 10.4

The Caddo madtom is a moderately elongate, slender madtom of the subgenus *Rabida* and is easily mistaken for the brindled madtom, *Noturus miurus* (Robison and Buchanan 1988). It has thirteen to sixteen anal rays and nine, sometimes ten, pelvic rays. This endemic madtom is most similar to the brindled madtom, but it differs by possessing shorter spines with smaller serrae, a shorter posterior process of the cleithrum, and dark pigment in the basal half of the adipose fin that only rarely extends to the margin, versus a black blotch extending to the margin of the adipose fin in *N. miurus*. It differs from the mountain madtom, *N. eleutherus*, by having a more adnate adipose fin and more prominent saddles, and it varies from the Ozark madtom, *N. albater*, by having eight soft pectoral rays, a submarginal adipose bar, and no prominent basicaudal band (Douglas 1972).

The Caddo madtom typically inhabits shallow gravel-bottomed pools of clear upland streams. It prefers well-compacted gravel areas below gravel riffles,

where it lives under rocks and large gravel and in the interstices of rubble (Robison and Harris 1978).

Foods include snails, isopods, mayflies, dragonflies, caddisflies, stoneflies, aquatic lepidopterans, aquatic beetles, and dipterans. Ephemeropterans and dipterans are dominant food items.

Spawning occurs from late April to May; however, no nests have been found. Ova counts from ripe females range up to forty-eight mature eggs but average sixteen eggs per female (Robison and Buchanan 1988). Due to continuing habitat loss, this rare catfish species should be considered threatened.

TYPE DEPOSITORY. Holotype: United States National Museum.
TYPE LOCALITY. Arkansas: Montgomery County; South Fork of Caddo River, 1.6 km SE of Hopper and 0.8 km S of Hwy. 240. Date: 5 March 1971. Collectors: N. H. Douglas, S. W. Fruge, D. Head, and J. Lindley.
DISTRIBUTION. Arkansas: Montgomery, Pike, Polk.

FIG. 10.4. *Noturus taylori*, Caddo madtom, endemic to the Ouachita Mountains of Arkansas. *Photograph by Bruce Bauer.*

Etheostoma moorei Raney and Suttkus 1964: 131

Yellowcheek Darter

FIGURES 10.5, 10.6

The yellowcheek darter is a small darter with a moderately sharp snout, a compressed, deep body, and a deep caudal peduncle. It is similar to the yolk darter, *E. juliae*, but can be distinguished by its separate to narrowly joined gill membranes, its naked nape (versus fully scaled), and its lack of a wide, dark saddle anterior beginning at the first dorsal fin and extending down to both pectoral fin bases.

The yellowcheek darter lives in the swift to moderate riffles occurring over gravel, rubble, and boulder substrates in the high-gradient headwater streams of the Little Red River system. Although juvenile individuals are found in shallow riffles, adults commonly occur at depths of ten to twenty inches. Raney and Suttkus (1964) reported the aquatic plant *Podostemon* often growing in the riffles where this species was taken from.

Foods consist primarily of aquatic dipteran larvae (Chironomidae and Simuliidae), but stoneflies, mayflies, and caddisflies were also eaten (McDaniel 1984). McDaniel (1984) reported that spawning of this darter occurred from late May through June in the swifter portions of riffles around or under the largest substrate particles available. Little else is known about the yellowcheek darter's spawning behavior, egg deposition sites, territoriality, or nest defense. Sexual maturity of males and females is reached at one year of age. Maximum life span is four years.

TYPE DEPOSITORY. Holotype: CU 42883, Cornell University.

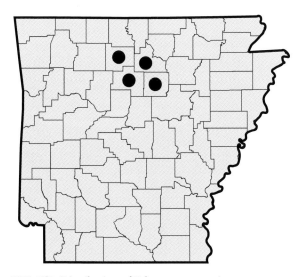

FIG. 10.5. Distribution of *Etheostoma moorei.*

FIG. 10.6. *Etheostoma moorei*, yellowcheek darter, endemic to the Ozark Mountains of Arkansas. *Photograph by William H. Roston.*

TYPE LOCALITY. Arkansas: Cleburne County; Devil's Fork of Little Red River, 4 km SW of Woodrow and 9.7 km W of Drasco. Date: 26 April 1962. Collectors: L. W. Knapp and R. V. Miller.

DISTRIBUTION. Arkansas: Cleburne, Searcy, Stone, and Van Buren.

Etheostoma pallididorsum Distler and Metcalf 1962: 556

Paleback Darter

FIGURES 10.7, 10.8

The paleback darter is a small slender darter with a distinctively wide pale stripe extending along the middle of the back from the head to the base of the caudal fin. This darter is similar to the the closely related but allopatric Arkansas darter, *E. cragini;* however, it differs in having a wide pale middorsal stripe, a more slender body, and a naked anterior belly (versus a fully scaled belly). Williams and Robison (1980) placed the paleback darter in the subgenus *Ozarka*.

Robison (1980) described the habitat of this darter as quiet shallow pools at the margins of small gravel-bottomed spring-fed streams and rivulets. The paleback darter avoids swift current and is often associated with vegetation growing over a mud substrate. Hambrick and Robison (1979) reported foods as being small crustaceans, mayfly larvae, and other immature aquatic insects. Maximum life span is two years. Sexual maturity is reached at one year of age. Spawning occurs in February and March. Unpublished studies by Robison found spawning of the paleback darter to occur in small seepage water in open pastures or wooded areas. Such spawning habitat differs from the nonbreeding habitat which usually includes small creeks where current is slow. Hambrick and Robison

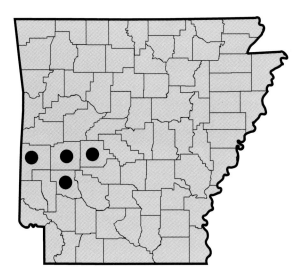

FIG. 10.7. Distribution of *Etheostoma pallididorsum*.

(1978) reported two hermaphroditic specimens (KU 6158) from Montgomery County.

TYPE DEPOSITORY. Holotype: KU 7144, Museum of National History, University of Kansas.
TYPE LOCALITY. Arkansas: Montgomery County; Caddo River, 13.7 km W of Black Springs. Date: 28 June 1961. Collectors: D. A. Distler and A. L. Metcalf.
DISTRIBUTION. Arkansas: Garland, Montgomery, Pike, Polk.

FIG. 10.8. *Etheostoma pallididorsum*, paleback darter, endemic to the Ouachita Mountains of Arkansas. *Photograph by John L. Harris.*

Etheostoma spectabile fragi Distler 1968: 162
Strawberry River Orangethroat Darter
FIGURE 10.9, 10.10

The Strawberry River orangethroat darter was described by Distler (1968). It is quite distinctive in

color pattern with a red throat, a little dark pigment in lateral vertical bars, and orange interspaces between the bars that are often continuous across the belly in a chevron-shaped pattern. The darters are abundant in small gravel-bottomed streams in the Strawberry River system that are high gradient and spring fed. Although no evidence of intergradation was found, Distler reluctantly described this form as a subspecies of *E. spectabile,* although later he reported that further study of this form might prove it to be specifically distinct (Distler, pers. comm. 1986).

TYPE DEPOSITORY. Holotype: KU 7481, Museum of Natural History, University of Kansas.
TYPE LOCALITY. Arkansas: Sharp County; Spring Creek, a tributary of Big Creek (Sec. 36, T16N, R5W). Date: 10 April 1963. Collectors: D. A. Distler and J. F. Downhower.
DISTRIBUTION. Arkansas: Fulton, Izard, Lawrence, Sharp.

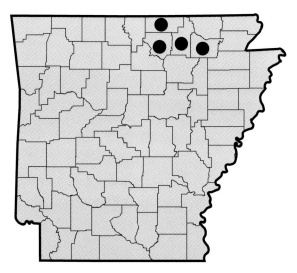

FIG. 10.9. Distribution of *Etheostoma spectabile fragi*.

FIG. 10.10. *Etheostoma spectabile fragi. Photograph by Henry W. Robison.*

11

Class Amphibia

Amphibians

Amphibians are members of the vertebrate class Amphibia. Herpetologists currently recognize about 3,250 species, and Arkansas is fortunate in having approximately 45 of them. Amphibians have been around since the Carboniferous, about 250 million years ago, when ancestral forms first ventured forth onto land from the security of the aquatic environment. Only two species of amphibians are endemic to Arkansas; both species are plethodontid salamanders and are limited to relatively small geographic regions within the state.

Family Plethodontidae— Lungless Salamanders

The plethodontid salamanders number approximately eighty species contained in eighteen genera. In Arkansas we have thirteen species in four genera. This successful group is believed to have evolved in the southern Appalachian Mountains; however, today they occupy the eastern half of North America, the west coast, Mexico, Central America, and South America.

The family gets its common name from the lack of lungs in adults. They take in oxygen through their skin and mouth lining. Plethodontids occupy a wide variety of habitats including springs, caves, and cold streams, as well as rock outcroppings and woodland areas with seepage.

Plethodon caddoensis Pope and Pope 1951: 148
Caddo Mountain Salamander
FIGURES 11.1, 11.2

The Caddo Mountain salamander was originally described by Pope and Pope (1951). They collected the

holotype and two paratypes of *P. caddoensis* at 1200 and 950 feet altitude in a mixed pine-oak forest on slopes with exposed rocky talus projecting through the soil.

P. caddoensis is quite similar to *P. ouachitae;* however, it lacks the chestnut pigment of the latter. *P. caddoensis* is also similar to *P. glutinosus,* but the whitish spots of *P. glutinosus* are more prominent and it has a dark throat. Blair (1957) compared the coloration of living specimens of *P. caddoensis* and *P. ouachitae.* Later Highton (1963) dealt with *P. caddoensis* in his revision of *Plethodon.*

Sexual maturity is reached at approximately 40 mm snout-vent length. Breeding habits and reproductive season are unknown.

TYPE DEPOSITORY. Holotype: 61959, Chicago Natural History Museum.
TYPE LOCALITY. Arkansas: Polk County; Polk Creek Mtn., elev. 1200 ft.
DISTRIBUTION. Arkansas: Howard, Montgomery, Polk.

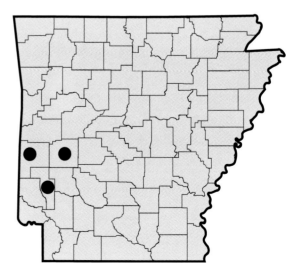

FIG. 11.1. Distribution of *Plethodon caddoensis.*

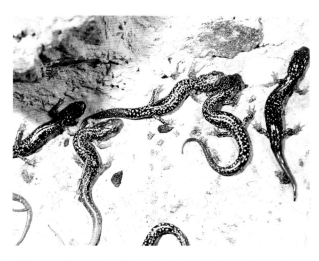

FIG. 11.2. *Plethodon caddoensis*, a lungless salamander endemic to the Ouachita Mountains of Arkansas. *Photograph by David A. Saugey.*

Plethodon fourchensis Duncan and Highton 1979: 109

Fourche Mountain Salamander

FIGURES 11.3, 11.4

Plethodon fourchensis is a large plethodontid species that is distinguished from all other *Plethodon* species by the possession of two longitudinal rows of large dorsal white spots. In addition, yellowish white spots are abundant on cheeks, legs, and sides. The chin is light. Costal grooves are sixteen. Maximum size is 73 mm snout-vent length. Females are generally larger than males.

Using the technique of starch-gel electrophoresis, Duncan and Highton (1979) elevated the Buck Knob variant of *Plethodon ouachitae* discussed by Blair and Lindsay (1965) to full species level, as *Plethodon fourchensis*; they hypothesized that *P. fourchensis* has been isolated from *P. ouachitae* for about a million and a half years. (See Duncan and Highton 1979 for a full discussion and evidence concerning elevation to species level.)

The Fourche Mountain salamander occurs in a mixed pine forest under talus and decaying logs.

TYPE DEPOSITORY. Holotype: USNM 204835, United States National Museum.
TYPE LOCALITY. Arkansas: Polk County; 1.5 km W and 0.3 km S of Wolf Pinnacle Mtn. summit. Date: 9 October 1976. Collectors: R. Beatson, S. B. Hedges, R. Highton, and D. M. Rosenberg.
DISTRIBUTION. Arkansas: Polk, Scott.

FIG. 11.4. *Plethodon fourchensis*, a lungless salamander endemic to the Ouachita Mountains of Arkansas. *Photograph by S. E. Trauth.*

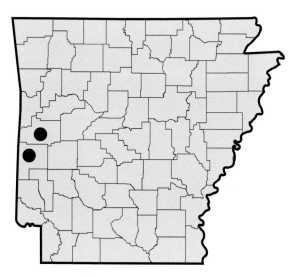

FIG. 11.3. Distribution of *Plethodon fourchensis*.

Literature Cited

Allen, R. T. 1988a. Additions to the known endemic flora and fauna of Arkansas. *Proc. Ark. Acad. Sci.* 42:18–21.

Allen, R. T. 1988b. A new species of *Occasjapyx* from the Interior Highlands (Insecta: Diplura: Japygidae). *Proc. Ark. Acad. Sci.* 42:22–23.

Allen, R. T. 1992. A new species of *Hanseniella* (Symphyla: Scutigerellidae) from the Interior Highlands of Arkansas. *Ent. News* 103 (5): 169–174.

Allen, R. T. 1993. A new species of *Podocampa* from the Interior Highlands of North America (Diplura: Campodeidae: Campodeinae). *Journ. Kan. Entomol. Soc.* 66 (3): 328–337.

Allen, R. T. 1994. Description of a new genus and species of Campodeidae from the Interior Highlands of North America (Diplura: Campodeidae). *Ann. Entomol. Soc. Am.* 87 (3): 270–276.

Allen, R. T., and C. E. Carlton. 1988. Two new *Scaphinotus* from Arkansas with notes on other Arkansas species (Coleoptera: Carabidae: Cychrini). *Journ. New York Entomol. Soc.* 96 (2): 129–139.

Allen, R. T., C. E. Carlton, and S. A. Tedder. 1988. A new species of *Acalypta* (Hemiptera, Tingidae). *Ark. Jour. Kansas Entomol. Soc.* 61 (1): 126–130.

Arkansas Department of Planning. 1974. *Arkansas Natural Area Plan.* Little Rock: Arkansas Department of Planning.

Arnett, R. H., Jr. ed. 1971. *The Beetles of the United States.* Ann Arbor, Mich.: The Amer. Entomol. Inst.

Ball, G. E. 1973. Carabidae. Chap. 4 in *The Beetles of the United States*, edited by R. H. Arnett, Ann Arbor, Mich.: The Amer. Entomol. Inst.

Bareth, C., and B. Conde. 1958. Campodeides endoges de L'Ouest des Etats Unis (Washington, Oregon, California, Arizona). *Bull. Soc. Linn. Lyon* 27:226–276; 297–304.

Barr, T. C., Jr. 1974. The eyeless beetles of the genus *Arianops* Brendel (Coleoptera, Pselaphidae). *Bull. Amer. Mus. Nat. Hist.* 154:1–51.

Barr, T. C., Jr. 1974. Revision of *Rhadine* LeConte (Coleoptera, Carabidae) I. The Subterranea Group. *Amer. Mus.* Novitates No. 2539:1–30.

Beaver, L. 1955. A new species of *Paraleptophlebia* from the southeast (Ephemeroptera: Leptophlebiidae). *Proc. Entomol. Soc. Wash.* 57 (5): 245–247.

Bedinger, M. S., and H. H. Hobbs Jr. 1965. Observations of a new troglobitic crayfish. *Bull. Nat. Speleol. Soc.* 27 (3): 93–96.

Blair, A. P., and H. L. Lindsay Jr. 1965. Color pattern variation and distribution of two large *Plethodon* salaman-ders endemic to the Ouachita Mountains of Oklahoma and Arkansas. *Copeia* 3:331–335.

Bollman, C. H. 1988. A preliminary list of the Myriapoda of Arkansas, with descriptions of new species. *Entomol. Amer.* 4:1–8.

Bouchard, R. W., and H. W. Robison. 1980. An inventory of the decapod crustaceans (crayfishes and shrimps) of Arkansas, with a discussion of their habitats. *Proc. Ark. Acad. Sci.* 34:22–30.

Bowles, D. E., and R. T. Allen. 1988. Description of the female of *Paduniella nearctica* (Trichoptera: Psychomyiidae). *Entomol. News* 99:7–9.

Candolle, A. P. de. 1830. Geographie botanique. *Dictionnaire des Sciences Naturelles.* Strasbourg and Paris, 18:359.

Carlton, C. E., and R. T. Allen. 1989. A new species of *Arianops* Brendel and the description of the male of *Arianops sandersoni* Barr (Coleoptera: Pselophidae). *Coleop. Bull.* 43 (1): 59–69.

Carlton, C. E., and R. T. Cox. 1990. A new species of *Arianops* from central Arkansas and biogeographic implications of the Interior Highlands *arianops* species (Coleoptera: Pselophidae). *Coleop. Bull.* 44 (3): 365–371.

Casey, T. L. 1893. Notes on the Coleoptera. *Ann. New York Acad. Sci.* 7:510–533.

Causey, N. B. 1950a. Two new polydesmoid diplopods. *Entomol. News* 61:37–39.

Causey, N. B. 1950b. Five new Arkansas millipedes of the genera *Eurymerodesmus* and *Paresmus* (Xystodesmidae). *Ohio Journ. Sci.* 50:267–272.

Causey, N. B. 1950c. A new genus and species of diploid (Family Xystodesmidae). *Chicago Acad. Sci. Nat. Hist.* 73:1–3.

Causey, N. B. 1950d. New genera and species of millipedes—Paraiulidae (Juloidea). *Proc. Ark. Acad. Sci.* 3:45–48.

Causey, N. B. 1950e. On four new polydesmoid millipedes. *Entomol. News* 61:193–198.

Causey, N. B. 1951a. On Eurymerodesmidae, a new family of Diplopoda (Stronglylosomidea), and a new Arkansas species of *Eurymerodesmus. Proc. Ark. Acad. Sci.* 4:69–71.

Causey, N. B. 1951b. The millipede assembly *Zinaria butlerii* isogen (Xystodesmidae). *Proc. Ark. Acad. Sci.* 4:73–88.

Causey, N. B. 1951c. New genera and species of chordeu-moid millipedes in the United States, and notes on some established species. *Proc. Biol. Soc. Wash.* 64:117–124.

Causey, N. B. 1951d. On two new colobognath millipedes and records of some established from east of the Rocky Mountains. *Proc. Biol. Soc. Wash.* 64:137–140.

Causey, N. B. 1952a. Some records and descriptions of polydesmoid millipedes from the United States. *Chicago
Acad. Sci. Nat. Hist.* 106:1–11.

Causey, N. B. 1952b. On three new eurymerodesmoid millipedes and notes on *Paresmus impurus* (Wood).
Entomol. News 63:169–176.

Causey, N. B. 1952c. Four chordeumoid millipedes from the
United States. *Proc. Biol. Soc. Wash.* 65:111–118.

Causey, N. B. 1953. On five new North American millipedes
and records of some established species. *Amer. Midl.
Nat.* 50:152–158.

Causey, N. B. 1954. Three new species and new records of
southern millipedes. *Tulane Stud. Zool.* 2:63–68.

Causey, N. B. 1955. New records and descriptions of polydesmoid millipedes (Order Polydesmida) from the eastern United States. *Proc. Biol. Soc. Wash.* 68:21–30.

Chamberlin, R. V. 1942. New southern millipedes. *Bull. Univ.
Utah, Biol. Ser.* 6:1–19.

Chamberlin, R. V. 1943. On nine North American polydesmoid millipedes. *Proc. Biol. Soc. Wash.* 56:35–40.

Chamberlin, R. V. 1958. List of the pseudoscorpions of
North America North of Mexico. *Bull. Amer. Mus. Nat.
Hist.* Novitates No. 1875.

Chamberlin, R. V., and R. L. Hoffman. 1958. Checklist of the
millipedes of North America. *Bull. U.S. Natl. Mus.* 212.

Chandler, D. S. 1988. A cladistic analysis of the world genera
of Tychini (Coleoptera: Pselaphidae). *Trans. Amer.
Entomol. Soc.* 114:147–165.

Conde, B. 1973. Campodeides Endoges de L'Est des Etats-
Unis. *Bull. Soc. Linn. Lyon* 42:17–29.

Conde, B., and P. Geeraert. 1962. Campodeides endoges du
centre des Etats-Unis. *Archieves de Zool. Expt. ent
Generale, Nancy,* 101:73–160.

Conde, B., and M. J. Thomas. 1957. Contributions a la faune
des Campodeides de Californie (Insectes Diploures).
Bull. Soc. Linn. Lyon 26:81–96; 118–127; 142–155.

Cox, C. B. 1974. Vertebrate paleodistributional patterns and
continental drift. *Journ. Biogeo.* 1:75–94.

Darlington, P. J. 1957. *Zoogeography, the Geographical
Distribution of Animals.* New York: John Wiley and Sons.

Distler, D. A. 1968. Distribution and variation of *Etheostoma
spectabile* (Agassiz) (Percidae, Teleostei). *Univ. Kansas
Sci. Bull.* 48 (5): 143–208.

Distler, D. A., and A. L. Metcalf. 1962. *Etheostoma pallididorsum,* a new percid fish from the Caddo River system of
Arkansas. *Copeia* (3): 556–562.

Douglas, N. H. 1972. *Noturus taylori,* new species of madtom (Pisces, Ictaluriade) from the Caddo River, southwest Arkansas. *Copeia* (4): 785–789.

Drake, G. J., and J. D. Lattin. 1963. American species of the
lacebug genus *Acalypta* (Hemiptera: Tingidae). *Proc.
U.S. Nat. Mus.,* no. 3486, 115:331–345.

Ducan, R., and R. Highton. 1979. Genetic relationships of
the eastern large *Plethodon* of the Ouachita Mountains.
Copeia 1:95–110.

Dyal, S. C. 1983. *Valerianella* in North America. *Rhodora*
40:185–212.

Fall, H. G. 1929. A new genus and species of Sytiscidae.
Journ. New York Entomol. Soc. 35:177–178.

Fitzpatrick, J. F. 1965. A new subspecies of the crawfish
Oronecetes leptogonopodus from the Ouachita River
drainage in Arkansas. *Tulane Stud. Zool.* 3:87–91.

Fitzpatrick, J. F., Jr. 1978. A new crawfish of the subgenus
Girardiella, genus *Procambarus* from northwest
Arkansas (Decapoda, Cambaridae). *Proc. Biol. Soc.
Wash.* 91 (2): 533–538.

Fleming, L. E. 1972. The evolution of the eastern North
American isopods of the genus *Asellus* (Curstacea:
Asellidae). *Int. Journ. Speleol.* 4:221–256.

Flint, O. S., Jr. 1967. The first record of the Paduniellini in
the New World. *Proc. Entomol. Soc. Wash.* 69 (4):
310–311.

Frazer, K. S., and S. C. Harris. 1991. Cladistic Analysis of the
Ochrotrichia shawnee Group (Trichoptera:
Hydroptilidae) and description of a new member from
the Interior Highlands of northwestern Arkansas. *Jour.
Kansas Entomol. Soc.* 64 (4): 363–371.

Freitag, R. 1969. A revision of the species of the genus
Evarthrus Leconte (Coleoptera: Carabidae). *Quaest.
Entomol.* 5 (2): 89–212.

Frierson, L. S. 1927. *A Classified and Annotated Check List of
the North American Naiades.* Waco, Tex.: Baylor
University Press.

Frison, T. H. 1934. Four new species of stoneflies from
North America (Plecoptera). *Canad. Entomol.* 46:25–30.

Gates, E. E. 1977. More on the earthworm genus *Diplocardia.*
Megadrilogica 3 (1): 1–47.

Gidaspow, T. 1973. Revision of ground beetles of the
American genus *Cychrus* and four subgenera of genus
Scaphinotus (Coleoptera: Carabidae). *Bull. Amer. Mus.
Nat. Hist.* 152 (2): 102.

Goodrich, C. 1939. Pleuroceridae of the Mississippi River
Basin exclusive of the Ohio River system. *Occ. Pap. Mus.
Zool., Univ. Mich.* 406:1–4.

Gordon, A. E. 1974. A synopsis and phylogenetic outline of
the Nearctic members of *Cheumatopsyche. Proc. Acad.
Nat. Sci. Phild.* 126:117–160.

Gordon, M. E. 1980. Recent Mollusca of Arkansas with
annotations to systematics and zoogeography. *Proc. Ark.
Acad. Sci.* 34:58–62.

Gordon, M. E., and J. L. Harris. 1985. Distribution of
Lampsilis powelli (Lea) (Bivalvia: Unionacea). *The
Nautilus* 99 (4): 142–144.

Gordon, M. E., and L. R. Kramer. 1984. *Lampsilis reeveiana*
and *Lampsilis streckeri* (Bivalva: Unionacea): some
clarifications. *Malacol. Rev.* 17:99–100.

Gordon, M. E., L. R. Kramer, and A. V. Brown. 1980.
Unionacea of Arkansas: historical review, checklist, and
observations on distributional patterns. *Bull. Amer.
Malacol. Union* for 1979:31–37.

Hambrick, P. S. , and H. W. Robison. 1978. An
hermaphroditic paleback darter, *Etheostoma pallididorsum,* with notes on other aberrant darters. (Percidae).
Southwestern Nat. 23 (1): 170–171.

Hambrick, P. S., and H. W. Robison. 1979. Life history aspects of the paleback darter *Etheostoma pallididorsum* (Pisces: Percidae) in the Caddo River system, Arkansas. *Southwestern Nat.* 24 (3): 475-484.

Harris, J. L., and M. E. Gordon. 1987. Distribution and status of rare and endangered mussels (Mollusca: Margaritiferidae, Unionidae). *Proc. Ark. Acad. Sci.* 41:49–56.

Hermann, F. J. 1972. A new variety of *Carex bicknellii* from Arkansas. *Sida* 5 (1): 49.

Herman, L. H., Jr. 1972. A revision of the rove-beetle genus *Charhyphus* (Coleoptera, Staphylinidae, Phloeocharinae). *Amer. Mus.* Novitates No. 2496:1–16.

Hess, W. J. 1989. Letter to Richard W. Davies, Director, Arkansas State Parks, dated 21 December 1989.

Hickman, et al. 1988. *Integrated Principles in Zoology.* St. Louis: Mosby Publ.

Highton, R. 1962. Revision of North American Salamanders of the genus *Plethodon. Bull. Fla. State Mus.* 6:235–367.

Hinkley, A. A. 1916. New fresh-water shells from the Ozark Mountains. *Proc. U. S. Nat. Mus.* 49:587–589.

Hoff, C. C. 1945. New species and records of pseudoscorpions from Arkansas. *Trans. Amer. Micros. Soc.* 64:34–57.

Hobbs, H. H., Jr. 1969. On the distribution and phylogeny of the crayfish genus *Cambarus.* In *The Distributional History of the Biota of the Southern Appalachians.* Pt 1 of *Invertebrates,* edited by P. C. Holt, R. L. Hoffman, and C. W. Hart Jr. Blacksburg: Virginia Polytechnic Institute, Research Division Monogr. 1.

Hobbs, H. H., Jr. 1973. New species and relationships of the members of the genus *Fallicambarus. Proc. Biol. Soc. Wash.* 86 (40): 461–482.

Hobbs, H. H., Jr. 1977. The crayfish *Bouchardinaa robisoni,* a new genus and species (Decapoda, Cambaridae) from southern Arkansas. *Proc. Biol. Soc. Wash.* 89 (2): 733–742.

Hobbs, H. H., Jr. 1979. A new crayfish from the Ouachita River Basin in Arkansas (Cambaridae: Decapods). *Proc. Biol. Soc. Wash.* 92 (4): 804–811.

Hobbs, H. H., Jr., and M. S. Bedinger. 1964. A new troglobitic crayfish of the genus *Cambarus* (Decopoda, astacidae) from Arkansas with a note on the range of *Cambarus cryptodytes* Hobbs. *Proc. Biol. Soc. Wash.* 100 (4): 1040–1048.

Hobbs, H. H., Jr., and A. V. Brown. 1987. A new troglobitic crayfish from northwestern Arkansas (Decapoda: Cambaridae). *Proc. Biol. Soc. Wash.* 100 (4): 1040–1048.

Hobbs, H. H., Jr., and H. W. Robison. 1985. A new burrowing crayfish (Decopoda: Cambaridae) from southwestern Arkansas. *Proc. Biol. Soc. Washington* 98(4):1035–1041.

Hobbs, H. H., Jr., and H. W. Robison. 1988. The crayfish subgenus *Girardiella* (Decapoda: Cambaridae) in Arkansas, with the descriptions of two new species and a key to the members of the *gracilis* group in the genus *Procambarus. Proc. Biol. Soc. Wash.* 101 (2): 391–413.

Hobbs, H. H., Jr., and H. W. Robison. 1989. On the crayfish genus *Fallicambarus* (Decapoda: Cambaridae) in Arkansas, with notes on the *fodiens* complex and descriptions of two species. *Proc. Biol. Soc. Wash.* 102 (3): 651–697.

Hoff, C. C., and J. E. Bolsterti. 1956. Pseudoscorpions of the Mississippi River drainage basin area. *Trans. Amer. Micros. Soc.* 75:155–179.

Holsinger, J. R. 1967. Systematics, speciation, and distribution of the subterranean amphipod genus *Stygonectes* (Gammaridae). *U.S. Nat. Mus. Bull.* 259: 179.

Hubbs, C. L., and J. D. Black. 1941. The subspecies of the American percid fish, *Poecilichthys whipplii. Occ. Pap. Mus. Zool., Univ. Mich.* 42:1–21.

Hubricht, L. 1966. Some land snail records from Arkansas and Oklahoma. *The Nautilus* 79 (4): 117–118.

Hubricht, L. 1972. The land snails of Arkansas. *Sterkiana.* 46:15–17.

Hubricht, L. 1979. A new species of *Amnicola* from an Arkansas cave (Hydropbiidae). *The Nautilus* 94 (4): 142.

Hubricht, L. 1985. The distributions of the native land mollusks of the eastern United States. *Fieldiana* (*Zoology,* new series) 24:1–191.

Hubricht, L., and L. G. Mackin. 1940. Descriptions of nine new species of fresh-water amphipod crustaceans with notes and new localities for other species. *Amer. Midl. Nat.* 23:187–218.

Hubricht, L. and L. G. Mackin. 1949. The freshwater isopods of the genus *Lireus* (Asellota: Asellidae). *Amer. Midl. Nat.* 42 (2): 334–349.

Hunter, C. G. 1984. *Wildflowers of Arkansas.* Little Rock: The Ozark Society Foundation.

Johnson, R. I. 1980. Zoogeography of the North American Unionacea (Mollusca: Bivalvia) north of the maximum Pleistocene glaciation. *Bull. Mus. Comp. Zool.* 149:77–189.

Kral, R., and V. Bates. 1991. A new species of *Hydrophyllum* from the Ouachita Mountain of Arkansas. *Novon* 1 (2): 60–66.

Lagler, K. F., J. E. Bardach, R. R. Miller, and D. R. M. Passino. 1977. *Ichthyology.* 2d ed. New York: John Wiley and Sons.

Lewis, J. J. 1983. *Caecidotea fonticulus,* the first troglobitic asellid from the Ouachita Mountains (Crustacea: Isopoda: Asellidae). *Proc. Biol. Soc. Wash.* 98 (1): 149–153.

Maguire, B. 1951. Studies in the Caryophyllacea—V. *Arenaria* in America North of Mexico. *Amer. Midl. Nat.* 46 (2): 493–511.

Mathis, M. L., and D. E. Bowles. 1989. A new micro caddisfly genus (Trichoptera: Hydroptilidae) from the Interior Highlands of Arkansas, U.S.A. *Journ. New York Entomol. Soc.* 97 (2): 187–191.

Matta, J. F., and G. W. Wolfe. 1979. New species of Nearctic *Hydroporus* (Coleoptera: Dytiscidae). *Proc. Biol. Soc. Wash.* 92 (2): 287–293.

Mayden, R. L. 1985. Biogeography of Ouachita Highland fishes. *S. W. Nat.* 30 (2): 195–211.

McCafferty, W. P. 1977. Biosystematics of *Dannella* and related subgenera of *Ephemerella* (Ephermeroptera: Ephemerellidae). *Ann. Entomol. Amer.* 70 (6): 881–899.

McCafferty, W. P., and A. V. Provonsha. 1978. The Ephemeroptera of Mountainous Arkansas. *Journ. Kans. Entomol. Soc.* 51 (3): 360–379.

McDaniel, R. E. 1984. Selected aspects of the life history of *Etheostoma moorei* Raney and Suttkus. M.S. thesis, Arkansas State University, Jonesboro.

Mohlenbrock, R. 1985. Mount Magazine, Arkansas. *Natural History* 94 (10): 82–85.

Moore, D. M. 1939. *Delphinium,* a new species from the Arkansas Ozarks. *Rhodora* 41:193–197.

Nielsen, E. L., and O. R. Younge. 1938. Observations on the distribution of *Huechera arkansana* Rydberg. *Amer. Midl. Nat.* 19:595–597.

Nuttall, T. 1821. *A Journal of Travels into Arkansas Territory during the Year 1819, with Occasional Observations on the Manners of the Aborigines.* Philadelphia: T. W. Palmer.

Palmer, E. J. 1927. On Nuttall's trail through Arkansas. *J. Arnold Arb.* 8:52–55.

Palmer, E. J. 1942. The red oak complex in the United States. *Amer. Midl. Nat.* 27:732–740.

Peck, J. H. 1986. *Dryopteris carthusiana* at Mt. Magazine, Logan County, Arkansas. *Proc. Ark. Acad. Sci.* 40:94.

Pennak, R. W. 1978. *Fresh-Water Invertebrates of the United States.* 2d ed. New York, N.Y.: John Wiley and Sons.

Phipps, J. B. 1990. *Mespilus canescens,* a new rosaceous endemic from Arkansas. *Systematic Botany* 15 (1): 26–32.

Pilsbry, H. A. 1940. *Land Mollusca of North America (north of Mexico),* vol. 1 pt. 2. Monographs of the Academy of National Sciences of Philadelphia 3:575–994.

Pilsbry, H. A., and J. H. Ferris. 1906. Mollusca of the Ozarkian fauna. *Proc. Acad. Nat. Sci. Phila.* 529–556.

Pittman, A. B., V. Bates, and R. Kral. 1989. A new species of *Polymnia* (Compositae: Heliantheae) from the Ouachita Mountain region of Arkansas. *Sida* 13 (4): 481–486.

Pope, C. H., and S. H. Pope. 1951. A study of the salamander *Plethodon ouachitae* and the description of the allied form. *Bull. Chicago Acad. Sci.* 9:129–152.

Poulton, B. C., and K. W. Stewart. 1987. Three new species of stoneflies (Plecoptera) from the Ozark-Ouachita Mountain region. *Proc. Entomol. Soc. Wash.* 89 (2): 296–302.

Poulton, B. C., and K. W. Stewart. 1991. The stoneflies of the Ozark and Ouachita Mountains (Plecoptera). *Mem. Amer. Entomol. Soc.* 38:1–116.

Raney, E. C., and R. D. Suttkus. 1964. *Etheostoma moorei,* a new darter of the subgenus *Nothonotus* from the White River system, Arkansas. *Copeia* 1:130–139.

Reddell, J. R. 1983. A checklist and bibliography of the Japygoidea (Insecta: Diplura) of North America, Central America, and the West Indies. Texas Mem. Mus., Austin: Pearce Sellars Ser., No. 37: 41.

Rehder, H. 1932. Two new *Polygyras* from northern Arkansas. *The Nautilus.* 45:128–131.

Reimer, R. D. 1966. Two new species of the genus *Cambarus* from Arkansas (Decapoda, Astacidae). *Tulane Stud. Zool.* 13 (1): 9–15.

Ricker, W. E. 1952. Systematic Studies in Plecoptera. *Indiana Univ. Pubs., Science Series* 18:1–20.

Ricker, W. E., and H. H. Ross. 1969. The genus *Zealeuctra* and its position in the family Leuctridae (Plecoptera: Insecta). *Canad. Zool.* 47:1113–1127.

Robison, H. W. 1974. An additional population of *Etheostoma pallidiorsum* Distler and Metcalf in Arkansas. *Amer. Midl. Nat.* 91 (2): 478–479.

Robison, H. W. 1980. *Etheostoma pallididorsum* Distler and Metcalf, paleback darter. In *Atlas of North American Freshwater Fishes,* edited by D. S. Lee et al. Raleigh, N. C.: State Mus. Nat. Hist.

Robison, H. W., and T. M. Buchanan. 1988. *Fishes of Arkansas.* Fayetteville: University of Arkansas Press.

Robison, H. W., and G. L. Harp. 1985. Distribution, habitat, and food of the Ouachita madtom (*Noturus lachneri* Ictaluridae), a Ouachita River endemic. *Copeia* 1:216–220.

Robison, H. W., and J. L. Harris. 1978. Notes on the habitat and zoogeography of *Noturus taylori* (Pisces, Ictaluridae). *Copeia* 3:548–550.

Robison, H. W., and M. Schram. 1987. Checklist of the aquatic Isopoda of Arkansas. *Proc. Ark. Acad. Sci.,* Ark. Biota Survey Checklist No. 48.

Robison, Henry W., and K. L. Smith. 1982. The endemic flora and fauna of Arkansas. *Proceed. Ark. Acad. Sci.* 36:52–57.

Robotham, C. D., and R. T. Allen. 1988. *Paraleptohphlebia calcarica,* n. sp. (Ephemeroptera: Leeptophlebiidae) from Western Arkansas. *Journ. Kans. Entomol. Soc.* 61 (3): 317–320.

Rosendahl, C. O., F. K. Butters, and O. Lakela. 1936. A monograph on the genus *Heuchera.* Minn. *Studies in Plant Science.* Vol. 2. Minneapolis: University of Minnesota Pres.

Ross, H. H. 1938a. Descriptions of Nearctic caddisflies (Trichoptera) with special reference to the Illinois species. *Ill. Nat. Hist. Surv. Bull.* 21 (4): 111–183.

Ross, H. H. 1938b. Descriptions of new leptocerid Trichoptera. *Ann. Entomol. Soc. Amer.* 31 (1): 88–91.

Ross, H. H. 1938c. Descriptions of new North American Trichoptera. Proceed. *Wash. Entomol. Soc.* 40 (5): 117–124.

Ross, H. H. 1941. Descriptions and records of North American Trichoptera. Trans. *Amer. Entomol. Soc.* 67 (1084): 35–126.

Ross, H. H. 1944. The caddisflies or Trichoptera, of Illinois. *Bull. Ill. Nat. Hist. Surv.* 23 (1): 1–326.

Ross, H. H. 1956. *Evolution and Classification of the Mountain Caddisflies.* Urbana: University of Illinois Press.

Ross, H. H. 1959. The relationships of the three new species of *Trianodes* from Illinois and Florida (Trichoptera). *Entomol. News* 20:39–45.

Ross, H. H. 1963. The dunesland heritage of Illinois. Circular 49, Illinois Nat. Hist. Sun.

Ross, H. H. 1964. New species of winter stoneflies of the genus *Allocapnia* (Plecoptera, Capniidae). *Entomol. News* 75 (7): 169–177.

Ross, H. H. 1965. Pleistocene events and insects. In *The Quarternary of the United States.* edited by H. E. Wright Jr. and D. G. Frey. New Jersey: Princeton University. Press.

Ross, H. H. 1967. The evolution and past dispersal of the Trichoptera. *Ann. Rev. Entomol.* 12:169–206.

Ross, H. H., and W. E. Ricker. 1964. New species of winter stoneflies, genus *Allocapnia* (Plecoptera, Capniidae). *Trans. Illinois Acad. Sci.* 57 (2): 88–93.

Ross, H. H., and W. E. Ricker. 1971. The classification, evolution, and dispersal of the winter stonefly genus *Allocapnia. Ill. Biol. Monogr.* No. 45.

Ross, H. H., and J. D. Unzicker. 1965. The *Micrasema rusticum* group of caddisflies. *Proc. Biol. Soc. Wash.* 78:251–258.

Ross, H. H., and T. Yamamoto. 1966. Two new sister species of the winter stonefly, genus *Allocapnia* (Plecoptera, Capniidae). *Entomol. News* 27:265–267.

Rouse, E. P., and L. N. Medvedev. 1972. Chrysomelidae of Arkansas. *Proc. Ark. Acad. Sci.* 26:77–82.

Sampson, F. A. 1894. A preliminary list of the Mollusca of Arkansas (exclusive of Unionidae). *Ann. Rept. Ark. State Geologist for 1891*:181–199.

Sanderson, M. W. 1946. A new genus of nearctic Staphylinidae (Coleoptera). *Journ. Kans. Entomol. Soc.* 19 (4): 130–133.

Sanderson, M. W., and A. Miller. 1941. A new species of ground beetle of the genus *Rhadine* from an Arkansas cave (Coleoptera: Carabidae). *Proc. Ark. Acad. Sci.* 1:39–40.

Schuster, R. W. 1959. A monograph of the Neartic Plagiochilaceae. Pt. 2. *Amer. Midl. Nat.* 62:350–359.

Sclater, P. L. 1858. On the General Geographic Distribution of the Members of the Class Aves. *Journ. Linn. Soc.* (Zool.) 2:130–145.

Small, J. K. 1903. *Flora of the Southeastern United States.* New York: New York Botanical Garden.

Small, J. K., and P. A. Rydberg. 1905. Saxifragaceae. *North Amer. Flora* 22 (2): 81–158.

Smetana, A. 1983. The status of the Staphylinid genera *Derops* Sharp and *Rimulincola* Sanderson (Coleoptera). *Entomol. Scand.* 14:269–279.

Smith, E. B. 1977. Notes on the Arkansas Saxifragaceae. *Proc. Ark. Acad. Sci.* 31:100–102.

Smith, E. B. 1978. *An Atlas and Annotated List of the Vascular Plants of Arkansas.* Fayetteville, Ark.: By the author, University of Arkansas.

Smith, E. B. 1979. A new variety of *Galium arkansanum* (Rubraceae) endemic to the Ouachita Mountains of Arkansas. *Brittonia* 31 (2): 279–283.

Smith, E. B. 1982. A new variety of *Cardamine angustata* (Crucifera) from the Ouachita Mountains of Arkansas. *Brittonia* 34 (4): 376–380.

Smith, E. B. 1988. *An Atlas and Annotated List of the Vascular Plants of Arkansas.* 2d ed. Fayetteville, Ark.: By the author, University of Arkansas.

Smith, H. L. 1959. The Japygidae (Diplura) of North America, 3. *Occasjapyx* Silvestri and *Hecajapyx* new genus. *Ann. Entomol. Soc. America* 52:363–368.

Smith, L. M. 1969. Japygidae of North America, 7. A new genus of Provalljapyginae from Missouri. *Proc. Biol. Soc. Wash.* 73:261–266.

Stark, B. P. 1988. *Nymphs of North American Stonefly Genera* (Plecoptera). Vol. 12. Philadelphia: Entomological Society of America.

Stark, B. P., and K. W. Stewart. 1973. New species and descriptions of stoneflies (Plecoptera) from Oklahoma. *Entomol. News* 84:192–197.

Stark, B. P., K. W. Stewart, and J. Feminella. 1983. New records and descriptions of *Alloperla* (Plecoptera: Chloroperlidae) from the Ozark Ouachita region. *Entomol. News.* 94:55–59.

Steyermark, J. A. 1963. *Flora of Missouri.* Ames: Iowa State Univ. Press.

Taylor, W. R. 1969. A revision of the catfish genus *Noturus* Rafinesque with an analysis of higher groups in the Ictaluridae. *U.S. Nat. Mus. Bull.* 282:1–315.

Traver, J. R. 1934. New North American species of mayflies (Ephemerida). *Journ. Elisha Mitchell Sci. Soc.* 50:189–254.

Tucker, G. E. 1974. Threatened native plants of Arkansas. In *Arkansas Natural Area Plan,* edited by W. M. Shepherd. Little Rock: Arkansas Department of Planning.

Tucker, G. E. 1976. A guide to the woody flora of Arkansas. Ph.D. diss., University of Arkansas, Fayetteville.

van der Gracht, W. A., and J. M. van Waterschoot. 1931. Permo-Carboniferous orogeny in south-central United States. *Bull. Amer. Assoc. Petrol. Geol.* 15:991–1057.

Walker, B. 1915. Apical characters in *Somatogyrus* with descriptions of three new species. *The Nautilus* 29 (4): 37–41; (5) 49–53.

Wallace, A. R. 1876. *The Geographical Distribution of Animals.* 2 vols. New York: publisher unknown.

Wells, E. F. 1984. A revision of the genus *Huechera* (Saxifragaceae) in eastern North America. *Syst. Bot. Monog.* 3:45–121.

Williams, A. B. 1954. Speciation and distribution of the crayfishes of the Ozark Plateaus and Ouachita Provinces. *Univ. Kansas Sci. Bull.* 36:803–918.

Index

Abernathy Spring isopod, 45
Acalypta susana, 92
Agapetus medicus, 105
Aliulus carrollus, 76
Allocapnia, 87
Allocapnia oribata, 88
Allocapnia ozarkana, 88
Allocapnia warreni, 87
Alloperla caddo, 89
Alloperla ouachita, 89
Amnicola cora, 37
Amphibia, 111
Amphibians, 111
Amphipoda, 43
Amphipods, 43
Annelid worms, 33
Arachnids, 79
Arenaria muriculata, 26
Arianops copelandi, 100
Arianops sandersoni, 6, 7, 99
Arkansas, geological history, 19
Arkansas, natural divisions, 16
Arkansas, physiographic regions, 16
Arkansas, river systems, 16
Arkansas alumroot, 28
Arkansas fatmucket, 40
Arkansas River Valley, 16
Arkhoma Basin, 16
Auturus florus, 67

Beech family, 29
Beetles, 93
Biogeography, 3
Bivalvia, 40
Bony fishes, 107
Bouchardina robisoni, 48
Browne's waterleaf, 30
Bryophyta, 25
Buttercup family, 27

Caddisflies, 102
Caddo madtom, 108
Caddo Mountain salamander, 111
Caecidotea fonticulus, 45
Caecidotea holti, 46
Calico Rock oval, 38
Cambala arkansana, 77
Cambarus aculabrum, 49
Cambarus causeyi, 50
Cambarus zophonastes, 51
Cardamine angustata var. *ouachitana,* 31
Carex bicknellii var. *opaca,* 26
Caryophyllaceae, 26
Catajapyx ewingi, 81

Channelled pebblesnail, 36
Cibularia profuga, 64
Clams, 40
Cleidogona arkansana, 72
Cleidogona aspera, 73
Clivocampa solus, 83
Coleoptyera, 93
Continental movement, 11
Cossatot leafcup, 32
Craspedosoma flavidum, 76
Crayfishes, 48
Crowley's Ridge, 18, 19
Crustaceans, 43
Cyperaceae, 26

Dannella provonshai, 85
Decapoda, 48
Delphinium newtonianum, 27
Derops divalis, 9, 10
Desmonus pudicus, 64
Dinosaur tracks, 22
Diplocardia meansi, 33
Diplocardia sylvicola, 34
Diplurans, 81

Earthworm, 33, 34
Ephemeroptera, 85
Etheostoma moorei, 109
Etheostoma pallididorsum, 109
Etheostoma spectabile fragi, 110
Eurymerodesmus angularis, 68
Eurymerodesmus, bentonus, 68
Eurymerodesmus compressus, 68
Eurymerodesmus dubius, 69
Eurymerodesmus goodi, 69
Eurymerodesmus newtonius, 70
Eurymerodesmus oliphantus, 70
Eurymerodesmus schmidti, 70
Eurymerodesmus wellesleybentonus, 71
Evarthus parasodalis, 97

Fagaceae, 29
Fallicambarus caesius, 52
Fallicambarus gilpini, 54
Fallicambarus harpi, 52
Fallicambarus jeanae, 53
Fallicambarus petilicarpus, 55
Fallicambarus strawni, 56
Fourche Mountain salamander, 112
Foushee cavesnail, 37

Galium arkansasum var. *publiflorum,* 31
Gastropoda, 35
Geological history, 19

Hanseniella ouachiticha, 63
Helicopsyche limnella, 105
Hemiptera, 92
Heuchera villosa var. *arkansana,* 28
Hydrophyllaceae, 30
Hydrophyllum brownei, 30
Hydroporus sulphurius, 98

Insecta, 81
Insects, 81
Isoperla szczytkoi, 90
Isopoda, 45
Isopods, 45

Lace bugs, 92
Lampsilis powellii, 40
Lampsilis streckeri, 41
Laurasia, 11
Leaf beetles, 102
Lema maculicollis ab. *inornata,* 102
Leuctra paleo, 92
Lirceus bicuspidatus, 47
Lirceus bidentatus, 47
Liverwort, 25
Lungless salamanders, 111

Magazine Mountain amphipod, 43
Magazine Mountain shagreen, 39
Maple-leaved oak, 13, 29
Mayflies, 85
Mesodon clenchi, 38
Mesodon magazinensis, 39
Mespilus canescens, 28
Microcreagris ozarkansis, 79
Microhabitats, importance of, 23
Millipedes, 63
Mimuloria davidcauseyi, 65
Mimuloria depalmai, 66
Mississippi Alluvial Plain, 18
Molluscs, 35
Moore's delphinium, 27
Mount Magazine supercoil, 37
Mussels, 40
Myriapoda, 63

Natural divisions of Arkansas, 16
Natural regions of Arkansas, 15
Noturus lachneri, 107
Noturus taylori, 108

Occasjapyx carltoni, 8, 9, 82
Ochrotrichia robisoni, 104
Ofcookogona alia, 73
Ofcookagona steuartae, 74
Okliulus beveli, 76
Oligochaeta, 33
Orconectes acares, 57
Oriulus grayi, 77
Osteichthyes, 107
Ouachita creekshell, 42
Ouachita madtom, 107
Ouachita Mountains, 16, 17
Ouachita pebblesnail, 35

Ouachitychus parvoculus, 100
Ozark Mountains, 15, 17
Ozark spiderwort, 4, 5
Ozark witch hazel, 4
Ozarkogona glebosa, 74
Ozarkogona ladymani, 74

Pachybrachis pinicola, 102
Paduniella nearctica, 9, 10, 102
Paleback darter, 109
Pangea, 11
Paraleptophlebia calcarica, 86
Paravitrea aulacogyra, 37
Paresmus columbus, 71
Paresmus polkensis, 72
Paresmus pulaski, 72
Paucicalcarica ozarkensis, 103
Physiographic regions, 16
Plagiochila japonica ciliigera, 25
Plants, 25
Plecoptera, 87
Plethodon, distribution, 8
Plethodon caddoensis, 8, 111
Plethodon fourchensis, 8, 112
Plethodon glutinosus complex, 3, 4
Pleuroloma mirbilia, 66
Podocampa inveterata, 83
Polygyra peregrina, 38
Polymnia cossatotensis, 32
Polyzonium bikermani, 78
Predaceous diving beetles, 98
Procambarus ferrugineus, 57
Procambarus liberorum, 59
Procambarus regalis, 59
Procambarus reimeri, 59
Pselaphidae, 99
Pseudoscorpions, 79
Pseudozaona occidentalis, 79

Queen snake, 4, 6
Quercus shumardi var. *acerifolia,* 13, 29

Ranunculaceae, 27
Regina septemvittata, 4, 6
Rhadine ozarkensis, 97
Rich Mountain amphipod, 44
Rosaceae, 28
Rose family, 28

Sandwort, 26
Saxifragaceae, 28
Saxifrage family, 28
Scaphinotus, 8
Scaphinotus (Nomaretus) infletus, 95
Scaphinotus parisiana, 6, 7, 95
Sedge, 26
Segmented worms, 33
Shagbark hickory, 4
Short-winged mold beetles, 99
Snails and slugs, 35
Somatogyrus amnicoloides, 35
Somatogyrus crassilabris, 36
Somatogyrus wheeleri, 36

Speckled pocketbook, 41
Spermatophyta, 26
Stern's medlar, 28
Stoneflies, 87
Strawberry River orangethroat darter, 110
Stygobromus elatus, 43
Stygobromus montanus, 44
Symphylans, 63

Thicklipped pebblesnail, 36
Tiganogona moesta, 75
Toothwort, 31
Trichoptera, 102
Trigenotyla parca, 75

Villosa arkansasensis, 42

West Gulf Coast Plain, 17, 18
White liptooth, 38
Winter stoneflies, 87

Yellowcheek darter, 109
Yellowwood, 4, 5

Zealeuctra wachita, 91
Zoological realms, 3